G

UNIDENTIFIED FLYING OBJECTS

Unidentified Flying Objects

by Gene and Clare Gurney

illustrated with photographs

Abelard-Schuman
London New York Toronto

Library of Congress Catalogue Card Number: 75-105262
Standard Book Number: 200.71677.8
First published in Great Britain in 1971

The authors wish to thank the United States Air Force
for their permission to use the photographs which appear
on pages 49, 50, 66, 131, 132, 133 and 135; NASA for
the photographs on pages 98, 111, and 113; and United Press
International for the photographs on pages 81 and 89.

London	*New York*	*Toronto*
Abelard-Schuman	Abelard-Schuman	Abelard-Schuman
Limited	Limited	Canada Limited
8 King St.	257 Park Avenue S.	200 Yorkland Blvd.
WC2	10010	425
An INTEXT Publisher		

Printed in the United States of America

Contents

Illustrations

1

The
First Flying
Saucers

What is sometimes called the modern age of the flying saucer began on June 24, 1947. The day was warm and clear in the state of Washington where Kenneth Arnold, a thirty-two-year-old salesman for a fire-control equipment company, decided to take advantage of the good weather to fly from Chehalis to Yakima in a private plane.

When he took off from the Chehalis airport, flying saucers meant nothing to Arnold; he had never heard of them. Moreover, he had something else to occupy his attention. Airport officials at Chehalis had asked him to look for the wreckage of a C-54 military transport that had disappeared in the vicinity of Mount Rainier. This was a request often made of pilots whose flight plan carried them near the area where a missing plane might have gone down, and Arnold readily agreed to help out.

As he flew over the valleys and between the peaks of

Washington's Cascade Range, Arnold searched the ground beneath him hoping to spot the reflection of sunlight off the downed plane's wings or fuselage. He found no trace of the missing transport but as he flew between Mount Rainier and Mount Adams he saw something else.

It was about three o'clock in the afternoon when Arnold noticed a bright flash of light in the sky to his left. Then, to his amazement, he saw what appeared to be a chain of nine strange-looking aircraft approaching Mount Rainier. "I could see their outline quite plainly against the snow as they approached the mountain," he reported later. "They flew very close to the mountaintops, directly south to southeast down the hog's back of the range, flying like geese in a diagonal chainlike line, as if they were linked together."

As the startled pilot watched, the aircraft, if that was what they were, dipped or changed course slightly every few seconds, two or three of them moving at a time.

"They were approximately 20 or 25 miles away," Arnold recalled later, "and I couldn't see a tail on them. I watched for about three minutes . . . a chain of saucerlike things at least 5 miles long, swerving in and out of the high mountain peaks. They were flat like a pie pan and so shiny they reflected the sun like a mirror."

Arnold estimated that the objects were flying at about 9,500 feet and their speed was amazing. Arnold calculated it at almost 1,700 miles an hour. In 1947 that was at least three times faster than any known aircraft. "I never saw anything so fast," he said.

As Arnold watched, the silvery discs sped out of sight. Before they disappeared, however, he noted their positions on his map and the approximate time it took them to move from one location to another. After searching the sky in vain for another glimpse of the discs, the thoroughly puzzled Arnold flew on to Yakima.

Arnold's account of what he had seen created a sensation. Newspapers and magazines all over the country printed stories about the nine silvery discs that Arnold described as looking "like a saucer would if you skipped it across the water." Before long, reporters were referring to the discs as "flying saucers" and people everywhere were talking about them.

Many people, of course, scoffed at the idea of anything resembling a saucer flying through the air. Others were convinced that the flying saucers were a new secret weapon belonging to the United States or to the Soviet Union, and still others were sure that the saucers were spaceships from another planet.

Reporters were not the only ones who interviewed Kenneth Arnold. The U.S. Army Air Forces, soon to become the U.S. Air Force, was interested in his story, too. The mysterious flying objects might pose a threat to the security of the country. Until they were identified, no one could be sure they were harmless.

Soon after the sighting, a military intelligence expert called on Arnold, who described orally and in writing what he had seen on that eventful afternoon. The interviewer was impressed with Arnold's sincerity. He wrote in his report: "It is the personal opinion of the interviewer that Mr. Arnold actually saw what he stated that he saw. It is difficult to believe that a man of Mr. Arnold's character and

11

apparent integrity would state that he saw objects and write up a report to the extent that he did if he did not see them. To go further, if Mr. Arnold can write a report of the character that he did while not having seen the objects that he claimed he saw, it is the opinion of the interviewer that Mr. Arnold is in the wrong business, that he should be writing Buck Rogers fiction."

Not everyone was convinced, however. Kenneth Arnold had stated that the discs were from 45 to 50 feet long. Experts pointed out that at his estimated distance of 20 to 25 miles, Arnold could not have seen a 50-foot object. Either the discs were much closer to his plane or Arnold had greatly underestimated their size. Furthermore, he could not possibly have seen an object that was traveling as fast as he said the discs were traveling. But he had seen something. What was it?

One by one, the military intelligence experts considered and eliminated the possibilities. The discs weren't conventional aircraft. Neither were they some new kind of aircraft or weapon undergoing a secret test. There was no evidence that the discs were spaceships visiting the earth from another planet. And Arnold hadn't described an unusual cloud formation. Finally, the experts had the answer: Kenneth Arnold had seen a mirage caused by unusual atmospheric conditions on the day that he flew from Chehalis to Yakima.

But Arnold disagreed. He was an experienced pilot and a careful observer. "I am absolutely certain of what I saw," he insisted.

Kenneth Arnold wasn't the first person to see discs or other strange objects in the sky. There are written reports of mysterious flying objects that date back more than three thousand years and some of them are based on legends that are even older. It has been suggested that the accounts of glowing lights, fiery chariots and strange clouds that appear in the Bible may have been inspired by the sight of something unusual moving across the sky. In the Old Testament, for example, the prophet Ezekiel describes "a great cloud and a fire unfolding itself" that he saw coming out of the north. The literature of other religions also mentions unusual celestial objects.

Romans living before the time of Christ reported seeing a round object that looked like a globe or shield move across the sky from west to east. Another report tells of a fiery globe that fell to earth and appeared to become larger. After a few minutes it rose again and moved toward the east. The globe was brighter than the sun.

In A.D. 80, Roman soldiers stationed in Scotland reported seeing bright flames in the sky on a winter night and on several occasions they saw something that looked like a ship moving swiftly across the heavens. And in A.D. 98, at Rome, an object that resembled a burning shield crossed the sky from west to east.

Because these mysterious sightings and others like them were recorded by historians who lived many years later, few details have survived. The Romans may have seen the northern lights, bright stars or meteors that became fiery globes or ships or shields with much retelling. However, during the Middle Ages, when reporting was better, similar accounts were recorded. A writer known as Matthew of Paris tells us that in 1239 in England what appeared to be a very large, bright star rose in the southern sky one evening. It traveled slowly toward the north where it disappeared. The same writer also reports that a few years later the monks at St. Albans in England saw a large ship in the sky. It appeared to be a well-equipped ship made of planks.

Another medieval writer, Robert of Reading, tells of a fiery shape, the size of a small boat, that was seen crossing the English sky from south to north in 1323. Observers noted that when a bright red flame burst from the front of the object, its speed increased. After it disappeared, they heard loud noises in the distance. Other medieval writers have also recorded reports of bright lights, balls, discs and strange shapes that appeared in the sky to puzzle those who saw them.

In 1644 there was a report of a sighting at sea when sailors on a Spanish merchant vessel observed several bright, glowing objects in the nighttime sky. As the startled sailors watched, the objects broke formation and moved erratically. Then they resumed their formation and streaked out of sight.

What may be a firsthand report of a sighting comes from John Evelyn, an English writer who lived during the seventeenth century. In his diary he described what he called a "shining cloud" that appeared over southern England in March, 1643: "I must not forget what amazed us exceedingly the night before, namely, a shining cloud in the air, in shape resembling a sword, the point reaching to the north; it was as bright as the moon, the rest of the sky being serene. It began about eleven at night, and vanished not till about one, being seen by all the south of England."

Another strange sight in the skies above London was reported by a member of a British scientific society. On the evening of December 16, 1742, he observed a large, brightly lighted, cylinder-shaped object that moved slowly above the city in a northwesterly direction. It had a lighted tail and when first seen low on the horizon, it resembled a rocket. Strange flying objects similar to those seen in England were observed in other countries as well. There were reports of silvery or glowing discs in the skies over Ireland and Italy. Globes and other shapes were seen above Portugal, Scotland, France and Switzerland.

Two of the earliest reports of mysterious objects in the skies above the United States were recorded in 1833. That year a brightly lighted, hooklike shape was seen over Ohio and a large glowing object startled the residents of Niagara Falls, New York. In 1846, Lowell, Massachusetts, was visited by a big flying disc. It was reported to have dropped a lump of "fetid-smelling jelly."

Some of the best documented of the early American sightings occurred during the spring of 1897 when newspapers carried an unusually large number of stories about mysterious flying objects. On March 29, citizens of Omaha, Nebraska, saw a brightly lighted object in the sky which they said was "too big for a balloon." It sailed directly over the city. The next day a farmer who lived near Sioux City, Iowa, claimed that he was dragged several yards after being caught by a hook dangling from a craft similar to the one seen in Omaha. It, or one like it, reappeared over Omaha on April 6. This time the object was described as having what looked like a steel body, 12 to 15 feet long. By April 9 the mysterious craft had moved to Mt. Carroll, Illinois. That same day at Wau-

15

sau, Wisconsin, hundreds of persons said they saw an egg-shaped object with bright lights in the sky.

During the next few days, reports of strange objects in the sky came from several other midwestern states. Before the month was over, similar reports had also been received from Texas, Washington, D.C. and Virginia. The objects were usually described as "cigar-shaped" and equipped with flashing red, green and sometimes white lights.

Could the objects have been balloons? Possibly, although balloons cannot travel against the direction of the wind. Moreover, most of the observers described cigar-shaped, egg-shaped or conical craft, not round balloons. Dirigibles have to be ruled out because it wasn't until 1903 that the first successful one flew in the United States.

World War II produced another mystery. In 1944 British and American pilots began to see strange balls of fire when they were flying high-altitude missions against Germany. The pilots called the balls, which sometimes appeared singly and sometimes in formations of as many as 15 or 20, "foo-fighters" or "Kraut fireballs." They flew off the wingtips of the Allied planes or followed them at a distance, and they seemed to have no trouble keeping up with the fast, high-flying fighters and bombers. Pilots reported that even when they flew into cloud banks or went into power dives, the foo-fighters continued to follow them.

The mysterious flying balls were described as being very bright or glowing. Some were red, others were orange or golden. From time to time they appeared to wink their lights and change color.

In 1944 almost every Allied soldier and airman had heard

stories about secret weapons that Germany was developing in a frantic effort to avoid defeat. It was only natural, therefore, that many of the pilots who saw foo-fighters thought they had encountered one of the enemy's new secret weapons. Oddly enough, there were no reports of foo-fighters damaging planes although they did frighten the men who saw them. Since the new weapon did not engage in combat, the airmen decided that it must have been sent up to confuse Allied radar or perhaps to interfere electronically with Allied planes.

A few months after they first appeared in Europe, foo-fighters were spotted in the Far East by the crews of the B-29 bombers that were attacking Japan. They described glowing balls that winked their lights from red to orange to white and back to red as they followed the big planes. Like their fellow airmen in Europe, the B-29 crews found that it was impossible to outdistance the foo-fighters. No matter how fast the B-29 flew, or how many times it changed course, the foo-fighter would maintain its position until suddenly it vanished.

Had the Germans shared their new secret weapon with the Japanese? Or had Japan developed a secret weapon of its own? There was much speculation on the subject, all of it wrong, as it turned out. After the war, American intelligence officers learned that German and Japanese pilots had also encountered foo-fighters. They were as mystified as their American and British counterparts and, like them, assumed that the strange glowing balls must be a secret weapon developed by the enemy.

There were other explanations for the foo-fighters, of

course. One was that the airmen had seen St. Elmo's fire, the flamelike glow that accompanies the discharge of atmospheric electricity. Such discharges often take place along the wingtips and other exposed parts of aircraft. It was also suggested that the airmen, weary from long hours of wartime flying, may have seen nothing at all. Their nerves may have played tricks on them. Most explanations, however, favored St. Elmo's fire or something closely related to it. But no one could be absolutely sure, a situation that was also going to be true of many other strange things seen in the sky.

2
Three Saucer Classics

Stories about the World War II foo-fighters were revived after Kenneth Arnold reported seeing the nine flying saucers near Mount Rainier. And during the next few months several other people announced that they, too, had seen a flying saucer. Most of these claims received scant attention because the claimants could supply little information. On January 7, 1948, however, there was a sighting that involved several people, one of them fatally.

The incident began in Maysville, Kentucky, where several residents saw what appeared to be a strange-looking aircraft pass over the town. Because they had never seen anything like it before, they called the Kentucky State Highway Patrol. The Highway Patrol in turn called the nearest Air Force base which was Godman, located near Louisville. Did Godman know anything about the strange-looking craft that had been sighted at Maysville? Godman didn't, but the men in its control tower said they would watch for it.

About twenty minutes later the Highway Patrol called back. The plane, or whatever it was, had been seen at Irvington and Owensboro and they now had a better description of it. It was round and glowing, perhaps 250 or 300 feet in diameter and traveling rapidly westward.

Although the mysterious craft had evidently already passed north of Godman, the men in the tower continued their watch in case it reversed direction. The assistant tower operator was the first to see something. Was it an airplane? It did not look like one. Moreover, Godman had no report of a plane in the vicinity. Nor did it look like a weather balloon, either.

The tower alerted the base operations officer, the intelligence officer and the base commander. When they arrived, they were unable to identify the object; neither could several other officers who joined the group in the tower. The strange device appeared to be hovering over the field. It was large and looked metallic but it resembled nothing that anyone had ever seen before.

The mystery was still unsolved when a flight of four F-51s, led by Captain Thomas Mantell, approached Godman from the south. The planes, which belonged to the National Guard, were en route from Georgia to their air base near Godman. The F-51s were fast and already airborne. The puzzled men in the Godman tower, realizing that here was a chance to get a closer look at whatever was up there, called the flight commander. "Would Captain Mantell help them identify something they had sighted from the tower?"

Captain Mantell answered in the affirmative. One of his pilots was low on gas and would have to continue to his base; the three others would investigate. From his position, however, Mantell could see nothing. He requested a heading and was directed toward the south. Followed by his wingmen, Mantell turned south and began to climb. He was in radio communication with the tower and with the two other pilots, but there is no exact record of what was said. However, Mantell did report that he saw an object above and ahead of him. He had then climbed to 15,000 feet.

Evidently, Mantell was the only one of the three pilots to see anything because one of his wingmen cut in to ask what they were looking for. The tower asked Mantell to describe what he saw.

There are various versions of Mantell's answer. According to one, he said: "It's above me and I am gaining on it. I'm going to 20,000 feet."

Another version has him saying: "I've sighted the thing. It looks metallic and tremendous in size. Now it's starting to climb." A few seconds later, Mantell announced that he was climbing to 20,000 feet.

Because the F-51s had been engaged in a low-level mission, they carried no oxygen. At 20,000 feet, oxygen would be needed; in fact, it should have been used at 15,000 feet, the altitude at which Mantell's two wingmen turned back after vainly trying to contact their leader. The Godman tower couldn't reach him, either. And the watchers in the tower had lost sight of whatever it was that Mantell was chasing.

Later that afternoon a search plane spotted some wreckage about 40 miles from Godman. It was Captain Mantell's F-51. The pilot was dead.

Once it became known that the crashed F-51 had been looking for the strange object seen over western Kentucky, rumors began to circulate. According to one story, the mysterious craft had caused the F-51 to disintegrate because Mantell flew too close. Another account of the crash claimed that Mantell's body had never been found; he had been spirited away by the crew of a spaceship. In another version, the pilot's body was found but it was full of mysterious holes. And there were stories of radioactive wreckage and strange weapons.

The United States Air Force, which carefully investigates all accidents in which its aircraft are involved, rushed technicians to the scene of the F-51 crash. After examining the wreckage, studying all of the available records and interviewing witnesses, the investigators concluded that Captain Mantell had flown too high without oxygen. When he lost consciousness, his plane had gone into a spiraling dive, lost a wing and crashed. However, the question of just what Captain Mantell was pursuing when he flew so high proved more difficult to answer.

To solve the mystery surrounding the fatal chase, the Air Force called on the experts at its Air Technical Intelligence Center at Wright-Patterson Air Force Base in Ohio. They suggested that the National Guard pilot had seen and attempted to chase the planet Venus. The observers on the ground had also seen Venus. This explanation failed to satisfy the skeptics who agreed that Venus would have been visible in western Kentucky that afternoon. But, they pointed out, it would have been far too dim in the bright sky to confuse anyone, and certainly not an experienced pilot.

Doubt about what Captain Mantell had seen continued, even after the Air Force amended its explanation to include the possibility that one of the high-altitude balloons used by the Navy in its Skyhook research project may have been responsible for some of the sightings in Kentucky and nearby states on January 7. Skyhook balloons, which were very large and visible over great distances, especially when the sun was shining, were sent aloft to gather data about winds and cosmic rays. Because the project was secret, very few people had heard about the balloons. A check of the records revealed that a Skyhook balloon might have been released at Clinton County Air Force Base, Ohio, on January 7. Moreover, winds that day would have carried the balloon over the areas where the strange object was seen in the sky. Unfortunately, the Skyhook records for January 7 could not be located. So, for many people the question remained: What had Captain Mantell been chasing when he flew to his death?

When reliable witnesses supply information about an unidentified flying object and official investigators cannot identify it beyond any doubt, the sighting becomes a "classic." The Mantell case is one of the famous classics in flying saucer lore. The Chiles-Whitted sighting is another.

Clarence S. Chiles and John B. Whitted were Eastern Airlines pilots. On the night of July 24, 1948, they took off from Houston, Texas, in a DC-3 for Atlanta, Georgia. It was a clear, moonlit night. The DC-3 was a few miles southwest of Montgomery, Alabama, when Captain Chiles noticed a red glow in the sky and directed his copilot's attention to what he called "a new Army jet job." In 1948 jet fighters were still new and somewhat of a curiosity, even to airline pilots.

The "new Army jet job" was approaching them from above and a little to the right. It was traveling very fast and heading directly for the DC-3. Fearing a collision, Chiles pulled to the left. Without diminishing its speed, the "jet" veered slightly and passed on the right. Then it pulled up sharply and disappeared into some clouds.

The two pilots had the brilliantly glowing object in sight for only ten seconds, but it was long enough for them to realize that it wasn't a military jet. They later described what they saw as a cigar-shaped, wingless aircraft, about 100 feet long. Its surface was smooth except for two rows of lighted windows. A dark-blue glow illuminated the bottom of the craft and red-orange flames shot out from its rear to a distance of about 50 feet. It made no sound.

Because of the hour (2:45 A.M.), most of the passengers on the DC-3 were asleep. One man, however, said he saw a bright streak of light that appeared and vanished almost at once.

An hour before the mysterious object appeared near the DC-3, observers at Robbins Air Force Base in Macon, Georgia, saw a brilliant light that passed overhead from north to south. And two military pilots flying near the Virginia-North Carolina state line saw what appeared to be a bright shooting star in the direction of Montgomery, Alabama, at approximately the same time that Chiles and Whitted encountered the strange aircraft.

The Air Force received reports on all of these sightings and its investigators went to work. They made a careful check of air traffic in the Montgomery area that night because Captain Chiles was convinced that the speeding object was under some sort of intelligent control. No other planes had been flying near Montgomery at 2:45 A.M., however, and there was no record of an experimental aircraft or rocket test that night.

When the investigators turned to a study of meteor reports for July, they had better luck. A large number of meteors had been observed in the Southeast during the week of July 23 to July 30. The sighting at Robbins Air Force Base and the one made by the two military pilots were both identified as meteors. And finally, the flying object that Chiles and Whitted had reported was tentatively identified as a meteor.

The Air Force investigators theorized that the two pilots had been startled and simply misinterpreted what they saw. Instead of a strange craft with two rows of lighted windows, they had seen an unusually bright meteor at least 50 miles from their plane. As it fell toward the earth, the glowing meteor was shooting off flaming gases. When it seemed to disappear into the clouds, it actually disintegrated.

It was a plausible explanation. An element of doubt remained, however, and the Chiles-Whitted sighting became a saucer classic.

A few months later a lieutenant in the North Dakota Air National Guard added another classic to the list. It was 9 P.M. on October 1, and already dark, when Lieutenant George F. Gorman called the control tower at Fargo for landing instructions after a cross-country flight. The tower replied with the information that a Piper Cub was coming in from the south. It would land first.

Following the tower's instructions, Gorman circled the field. He saw the Piper Cub below him, but he also saw a moving, blinking light, like a plane's taillight, that passed on his right. The tower hadn't mentioned a second plane in the landing pattern. Gorman called back. They were working only the Piper Cub and his own plane, the tower operators assured him.

Puzzled by Gorman's call, one of the traffic controllers went to a window in the south side of the tower. He saw both the Piper Cub and a clear white light that appeared to be moving in a northerly direction.

Gorman called the tower again. Instead of landing, he was going to fly closer to the mysterious light to find out what it was. Through his binoculars, the controller watched Gorman turn in the direction of a light that seemed to have no shape. He saw nothing more than the light but it did resemble a plane's taillight, as Gorman had suggested. When the pilot of the Piper Cub landed, he confirmed that description. He had seen what he assumed was the taillight of a plane traveling away from the airport. It was being pursued by an F-51.

Meanwhile, Lieutenant Gorman was having trouble closing in on the light. He had chased it from 1,000 to perhaps 7,000 feet, trying to turn into the light as he climbed. After one pass, Gorman had to dive to avoid what he thought would surely be a collision. However, the light cleared the F-51's canopy by about 50 feet and the chase continued.

26

Now, however, the light seemed to be on the attack. No longer blinking, it headed straight for the F-51, only to pull up at the last moment. Gorman followed it to 14,000 feet, as high as he could go. He estimated that the light was 2,000 feet above him. When it descended, the contest resumed. They were about 25 miles southeast of Fargo when the light made one last pass, climbed straight up and disappeared. Gorman returned to the Fargo airport and landed. During his 27-minute adventure, he had seen only a round white light from six to eight inches in diameter, but he was convinced that its movements were intelligently controlled.

As soon as they received word of Lieutenant Gorman's strange experience, Air Force investigators rushed to Fargo. One of the first things they did was examine Gorman's F-51 with a Geiger counter. The F-51 showed a slight radioactivity, but no more than planes normally do after flight.

In addition to Gorman, four other persons had seen the mysterious light: two tower operators, the pilot of the Piper Cub and his passenger. They all had observed a fast-moving light, but none of them saw all of the maneuvers that Gorman reported.

A check revealed that no other aircraft had been in the area at the time of the sighting, but a lighted weather balloon had been released at Fargo at 8:50 that night. Because the balloon had drifted west and northwest toward the airport, it seemed reasonable to assume that Lieutenant Gorman had seen and chased it.

Like the other classics, the Gorman sighting is still debated by students of saucer lore. Why hadn't Gorman, an experienced pilot, recognized the balloon? Would a balloon abruptly change course and appear to attack a plane? And what about Gorman's statement that the light's maneuvers seemed to be under some sort of intelligent control?

Because the balloon explanation fits some, but not all, the facts in the Gorman case, it has been suggested that he might have seen two different things: first, the weather balloon and then the planet Jupiter. And it has also been suggested that he saw and chased an intelligently guided spaceship.

Throughout the controversy, the Air Force has remained convinced that the lighted weather balloon released at Fargo is the best explanation of the Gorman sighting.

3

Project
Blue Book

At the time of the Chiles-Whitted and Gorman sightings, the U.S. Air Force, as the government agency responsible for investigating unidentified objects seen in the skies above the United States, had already begun a review of the many reports of unusual aerial phenomena that it was receiving from all parts of the country. The Air Force referred to the strange things seen in the sky as unidentified flying objects, or UFOs, a term which it defined to mean "any aerial phenomenon that the observer is unable to identify."

In 1948 the cold war with the Soviet Union was at its height. It was thought that some of the unidentified objects could be secret Soviet weapons. But the possibility that they might be of interplanetary or interstellar origin was by no means ruled out. In either case, there was a potential threat to the security of the United States.

The Air Force's Project Sign began operation on February 11, 1948. A year later, after carefully studying 243 sightings for which sufficient information was available, it issued a report. Project Sign's conclusion: "No definite evidence was available to confirm or disprove the actual existence of unidentified flying objects as new or unknown types of aircraft."

While the study was under way, the project's name had been changed to "Grudge," a designation, which, like the earlier "Sign," had no literal meaning. It was merely taken from a list of code names for classified, or secret, projects. Because the information developed from the study of UFO reports might be important to national security, both Sign and Grudge were secret projects. While it may have been necessary, this secrecy caused critics of the Air Force studies to claim that facts about UFOs were being withheld from the public. Neither Project Sign nor Project Grudge was staffed by trained scientists.

Project Grudge made a detailed study of 244 UFO sightings. Its report, issued in August 1949, explained 32 percent of the sightings as being astronomical phenomena; 12 percent were attributed to weather balloons; 33 percent were classified as hoaxes, airplanes or too vague to be explained; the remaining 23 percent were placed in the "Unknown" category. Project Grudge concluded: "There is no evidence that objects reported upon are the result of advanced scientific foreign development; and therefore they constitute no direct threat to national security." The report went on to suggest that the Air Force would be wasting time and money if it continued full-scale investigation of UFO reports.

Shortly thereafter, Grudge was discontinued as a separate project.

UFO sightings continued, however, and within a few months the public clamor for explanations produced another Air Force project to investigate UFOs. It was eventually named Project Blue Book, probably because of the blue covers on its reports.

Project Blue Book, which remained the official government agency for the investigation of UFOs until 1969, had a twofold assignment: to determine first, whether UFOs posed a threat to the security of the United States and second, if they exhibited any unique scientific information or advanced technology which might contribute to scientific or technical research. In carrying out its assignment, Project Blue Book tried to identify UFO sightings within the continental United States, or in areas of United States responsibility, which were reported directly to the Air Force or relayed to it by some law enforcement agency. The results of its investigations reached the public in the form of news releases, fact sheets and other publications issued by the Air Force Office of Information in the Pentagon.

What rules did Project Blue Book follow in its investigations? An Air Force regulation listed all the things that had to be done when a UFO was reported. The initial investigation was the responsibility of the commander of the Air Force base closest to the place where the UFO was seen. The commander did not investigate personally, of course. He sent a representative, usually an intelligence officer, who interviewed those who saw the UFO. He also asked them to fill out a questionnaire. That is what happened on the night of

July 11, 1959, when the crews of five commercial airplanes, all bound from California to Honolulu International Airport in Hawaii, reported seeing what appeared to be a cluster of lights speed across the sky. The lights were variously described as "one large light with four smaller lights to the left"; "one large light surrounded by a cluster of six or seven smaller lights"; "one bright center light with four smaller lights trailing it"; and "four white lights in a rectangle with a large bright light in the center." Some of the pilots said the lights were white; others said they were orange-yellow. But all of the reports agreed on the speed of the object. It was moving very rapidly, faster than any known aircraft.

When the five planes landed at the Honolulu airport, intelligence officers talked with the crews and gave them Project Blue Book's questionnaire to fill out. The questionnaire asked: When, where and for how long was the object seen? Was the object in sight continuously? What were the weather conditions? Did the object move behind or in front of something at any time? There were a number of questions about the size and appearance of the object and spaces for drawings.

If the lights could have been explained easily, the intelligence officers would have told the pilots what it was that they saw and closed the case. Because this UFO required further study, the investigators sent their reports and the completed questionnaires to Project Blue Book at Wright-Patterson Air Force Base where they were examined carefully.

Project Blue Book could call upon other government agencies and a number of scientists, scientific organizations and specialized businesses for whatever information and other help it needed in conducting its investigations. In this case, the Blue Book staff obtained data on the weather, the location of the moon and the stars that night and on planes, balloons and satellites that might have been in the area. As a final step the positions of the five planes involved in the sightings were plotted on a map and studied in relation to the reported movement of the mysterious lights.

After many hours of work, Project Blue Book had the answer. The pilots had seen a fireball, an unusually bright meteor which moved rapidly across the sky. If a fireball breaks apart, it appears as a cluster of lights. The unidentified flying object had been identified and was so listed in Project Blue Book files.

Between 1947, when Kenneth Arnold saw the silvery discs that he said resembled flying saucers, and 1969, more than 12,000 reports of unidentified flying objects were forwarded to Wright-Patterson Air Force Base. Excluding the reports for which not enough information was available, all but a small percentage of the 12,000 UFOs have been explained.

More than 2,000 of the 12,000 UFO sightings turned out to be planets, bright stars or astronomical phenomena of one sort or another. The fireball seen over the Pacific on July 11, 1959, falls into this category.

High-flying aircraft are often reported as UFOs, particularly when visibility is bad. The aircraft itself may appear to have a disc or globe shape and its vapor trail may look like a second UFO. Of the explained sightings in Project Blue Book files, 1,500 were aircraft.

As more and more man-made satellites circle the earth,

they figure in an increasing number of UFO reports. However, all satellites are carefully tracked by agencies whose records were readily available to Project Blue Book, and nearly 800 UFOs were identified as satellites launched by the United States or the Soviet Union.

Of the 12,000 sightings, 500 turned out to be balloons. A great many balloons, some of them very large and carrying lights, are released each day to gather information about the weather aloft or for other research purposes. The fact that information about balloon launchings and flight paths is available from the Weather Bureau and other sources has helped the Blue Book staff move balloon sightings into the "Identified" file.

Other UFOs in Project Blue Book's "Identified" file were explained as hoaxes, clouds seen under unusual conditions, flocks of birds, electrical discharges in the atmosphere, mirages and a host of common and uncommon phenomena.

In addition to its "Identified" file, Project Blue Book had a second file. It contained UFO reports that could not be explained because one or more important pieces of information were missing. Perhaps the person making the reports was unsure of the shape of the thing that he saw or the day on which he saw it. Or Project Blue Book may have received two or three conflicting reports of the same sighting. As long as there was hope of obtaining more information, the Project Blue Book staff continued to work on the cases in the "Insufficient Data" file and some of them were eventually explained.

Project Blue Book's third file was perhaps the most interesting one. It contained the small percentage of cases that could not be explained even though a considerable amount of reliable information was available. When the description of a UFO or its motion could not be identified as belonging to any known object or phenomenon, the sighting went into the "Unidentified" file.

A sighting at Washington, D.C., on the afternoon of December 13, 1961, is a good example of the kind of case that went into Project Blue Book's "Unidentified" file. George E. Weber, one of the three persons who saw the UFO, was crossing the George Washington University parking lot on his way to his car when a guard pointed out a strange object in the sky. The third observer, William John Meyer, Jr., was stopped at a traffic light when he noticed something odd flying through the air. When he got out of his car to obtain a better view, he saw what Weber and the university guard had seen: what was apparently a dark gray, diamond-shaped object, perhaps 20 feet long. It made no sound as it moved overhead at an altitude that appeared to be between 1,200 and 1,500 feet.

Weber later reported that he saw a light at the bottom of the object. Meyer, who was a former Navy pilot, described an orange-brown glow coming from the center area. He also noted the absence of wings, propellers or rotors although the object seemed to be moving through the air at a constant speed. It left no vapor trail in the cloudless sky.

The two observers in the university parking lot had the UFO in view for three minutes. Weber watched it for only one minute before it disappeared behind some buildings. By then the traffic light had changed to green and impatient motorists were honking their horns at his stopped car.

Here was a sighting by three reliable witnesses who had observed an identical object from two different locations. What they reported resembled no known aircraft or balloon. It could not be explained as a mirage, a planet or bright star, reflected sunlight, unusual cloud formations or any of the other things that are sometimes mistaken for UFOs. There seemed to be no good explanation for the sighting, so it went into Project Blue Book's "Unidentified" file.

Although it was not able to identify every UFO reported to it, Project Blue Book insisted: "No evidence has been received or discovered which proves the existence and intra-space mobility of extraterrestrial life." In other words, although some UFOs, like the one seen by the three men in Washington, could not be explained, there was no proof that they had come from another planet.

Not everyone agreed with Project Blue Book. Many people were convinced that "Unidentified" UFOs did come from other planets. Moreover, there were those who questioned some of the explanations in Project Blue Book's "Identified" file. The skeptics claimed that some of those sightings were really interplanetary or interstellar spaceships. Kenneth Arnold, it will be remembered, never did accept the explanation that he had seen a mirage and there are those who still insist that Captain Mantell was chasing a UFO, not Venus or a balloon, when he crashed.

Another controversial sighting that attracted a great deal of attention occurred in Washington, D.C., in 1952. It began shortly before midnight on July 19 when a radar operator in the Air Route Traffic Control section (ARTC) at Washington National Airport noticed seven strange blips, or targets, on his scope. Unlike an airport control tower which supervises landings and takeoffs, ARTC watches over air traffic some distance from the airport, telling pilots how high and in what direction to fly. ARTC radarmen work in a windowless room because all the information they need comes from their scopes.

Above the control center a revolving antenna transmits pulses of energy. If an object, such as an airplane, is within its range (100 miles in the case of Washington) the antenna receives an echo, or return, which is transmitted to the center's radarscopes in the form of a violet-colored spot of light, or blip. As the plane travels, the blip moves on the scope. By watching his scope, a radarman can tell not only where a plane is but also how fast it is traveling.

When the ARTC radarman saw the seven blips, his first thought was that a seven-plane formation was approaching Washington. But he had received no radio communications from the pilots and he was unable to make radio contact himself. Because this was an unusual—and possibly dangerous—situation, he called in the senior controller who suggested that perhaps the radar was reporting something that wasn't there. A technician checked the scope; it was in perfect working order.

The mystery was only beginning. The ARTC radar operators were experienced men who were thoroughly familiar with the movement of aircraft as it was recorded on their scopes. Now they watched with amazement as the seven unidentified blips put on a sudden burst of speed after loafing along at 100 to 130 miles an hour. The blips made seemingly impossible sharp turns and other erratic movements that no airplane could execute.

The puzzled senior controller called the airport control tower. The radarmen in the tower had also picked up the strange blips on their scopes. So had the radarmen at Andrews Air Force Base a few miles east of Washington. The blips, close together at first, had separated. Some of them appeared to have flown above the White House and the Capitol, an area that was closed to all air traffic.

While they were trying to identify the mysterious blips, the radar operators were handling the normal air traffic at Washington National Airport. Landings and takeoffs were few because of the late hour, but before long a departing pilot called ARTC to report that he saw lights he couldn't identify. "There's one—off to the right—and there it goes!" he exclaimed. ARTC had been tracking the plane and something that appeared to be flying on its right. Now the unidentified blip disappeared but the blip representing the plane remained on the scope. Before he got beyond the range of ARTC's radar, the pilot reported seeing six more lights.

A short time later another pilot radioed the control tower at National Airport that a strange light seemed to be following him. Radar operators in the tower and at ARTC were already tracking an unidentified blip that had appeared on their scopes behind a plane approaching the airport from the west. When the pilot called back to report that the light was leaving, the blip moved away from the plane on the radarscopes.

Still later that night, tower operators at Andrews Air Force Base reported they had seen a "huge fiery sphere" when radar showed that one of the UFOs should be just to the south. There were a number of other sightings from the ground as well, but the crew of an F-94 interceptor, called in to search the sky above Washington, saw nothing. However, the F-94 didn't arrive until shortly before dawn and by then all the mysterious blips had disappeared from the radar screens.

They were back again a week later. At 10:30 P.M. on July 26, radar screens at Washington National Airport began picking up the first of several slow-moving, unidentified blips. Still puzzled, but not quite as disturbed as they had been a week before, the radarmen began to track the blips. They also put in a hurry-up call for F-94s. When two interceptors arrived, however, the blips disappeared from the radarscopes.

Guided by the airport radar operators, the F-94 pilots crisscrossed the area where the UFOs were last reported. Visibility was good, but the aircrews saw nothing. After a thorough search, they returned to their base.

Not long after the F-94s left, the unidentified blips returned to the radarscopes at Washington National Airport. Another call went out for F-94s and again two planes responded. This time the blips remained on the scopes but they sped away whenever an interceptor approached. The men in one of the planes reported that they saw lights, but even when they flew at the F-94's maximum speed, they could not get close enough to see anything more. After twenty minutes of high-speed but unsuccessful pursuit, the F-94s left. The blips, still unidentified, remained on the radar screens until dawn.

Under big, black headlines, newspapers all over the country carried stories about the UFOs that had flown over the nation's capital. The fact that the UFOs had been tracked by radar, seen by ground observers and chased by pursuit planes convinced many people that something really had been up there and they were worried. Editorial writers demanded that the public be told if the Defense Department was trying out a new plane or weapon that could have been mistaken for a UFO. And if that wasn't the case, they wrote, the government should explain what had caused the sightings in Washington and similar ones in other parts of the country.

The Air Force assigned some of its best investigators to the Washington case. Because airport radar was involved, Civil Aeronautics Authority experts studied the radar returns. Both groups of investigators concluded that the radar returns as well as the visual sightings had resulted from a temperature inversion over Washington on the nights of the sightings.

When conditions are normal, air gets colder as altitude increases. The decrease in temperature is gradual, about five degrees for every thousand feet of altitude. Sometimes, however, layers of warm air get mixed up with the colder air so that a layer of cold air will have a layer of warm air above it. This is known as a temperature inversion and it is particularly apt to happen during warm summer weather if the ground cools rapidly at night.

The investigators explained that when a light ray travels through the air during a temperature inversion, its warm-air, or upper, side will move more rapidly than its cool-air, or lower, side because warm air is less dense than cold air. This causes the light ray to bend instead of traveling in a straight line. For an observer on the ground, the rays are bent downward as they approach his eye and he may see objects or lights that are on the ground apparently floating in the sky. On the other hand, for an observer in an airplane above the layers of unstable air, the rays are bent upward and the image of the moon or a bright star may appear to be below him.

Radar signals, which normally travel out in a straight line from an antenna, can also be bent by temperature inversions. When that happens, radar can pick up ground objects that are re-reflected back to the antenna to show up on radar screens as strange blips that are difficult to identify. If the object picked up by the radar is a moving one, such as a car, the blips will appear to travel at a high speed and make sharp turns. This also happens when the layers of air in an inversion are turbulent. Moreover, when the weather is hot and humid, as it was in Washington on the nights of the sightings, radar is more apt to pick up stray signals which the radarmen call "phantoms," "ghosts" or "angels."

Controversy over the temperature inversion explanation of the Washington National Airport sightings continues to this day. Critics point out that the airport radar operators were all experienced men who should have been able to distinguish between the sharp image produced on their scopes by an actual return and the blurred images that the scopes show when they pick up stray ground objects during a temperature inversion. The radarmen insisted that they had tracked sharp images on the nights of the sightings. Moreover, they had never seen blips that maneuvered as these did, no matter what the weather.

Other skeptics checked Washington weather records and discovered that the differences in temperature between warm and cold layers of air had been slight on the nights of the sightings. There was a surface inversion of 3.1 degrees Fahrenheit on the night of July 19 and 2.2 degrees Fahrenheit on the night of July 26, but some experts claim that the difference in temperature has to be at least five degrees Fahrenheit to produce blips on radar screens and more than five degrees to produce strong returns.

Those who refused to accept the temperature inversion explanation of the radar returns also doubted that temperature inversion explained the lights seen from the ground and from aircraft. They also questioned the suggestion that the visual observers had seen meteors or bright stars that were unrelated to the radar returns. Instead, they insisted, the visual observers had seen the lights of spaceships and the same spaceships had produced the mysterious blips on the radar sets at Washington National Airport.

4

The Civilian
Investigators

Many of those who questioned the temperature inversion explanation of the Washington National Airport sightings had also refused to accept Project Blue Book's explanations of previous UFO reports. They contended that the Air Force was either not investigating carefully enough or that it was withholding the truth for reasons of its own. And the truth, they maintained, was that UFOs were actually extraterrestrial spaceships.

Since 1947 believers in the spaceship theory have been collecting their own information about UFO sightings and they have organized several civilian groups to further their research. One of the best known of the groups is the National Investigations Committee on Aerial Phenomena, usually referred to as NICAP. It was organized in 1956 to investigate sightings of unidentified flying objects and to work for the release of more UFO information by the government. NICAP has more than 8,000 dues-paying members who are encouraged to supply information about UFO sightings in the form of firsthand reports or newspaper clippings.

NICAP investigations are carried out by members who are unpaid volunteers. Each investigating unit—NICAP calls them subcommittees—is advised by a scientist or technician. The subcommittees interview UFO witnesses, examine evidence and gather data on local conditions at the time of the sightings. NICAP also uses a questionnaire to obtain information about the UFO and the reliability of the person who saw it.

At its Washington headquarters, NICAP maintains an extensive file of UFO sightings. While Project Blue Book has repeatedly stated that its investigations have produced no evidence that UFOs are extraterrestrial vehicles, NICAP claims that some of the cases in its files indicate just the opposite. In 1964 the organization published *The UFO Evidence,* a compiliation of 746 sightings which, according to the NICAP board of governors, backs up the hypothesis that unexplained UFOs are real objects under some kind of intelligent control.

NICAP complains that Air Force investigation of UFOs has been unscientific in some cases and overly secretive in almost all cases. The reason for the secrecy, NICAP suggests, is either that the Air Force knows that UFOs are extraterrestrial but is not yet ready to inform the public or that government red tape and the lack of a clear policy have cut off information about UFOs. Some UFOs are extraterrestrial, says NICAP, and should be the subject of a continuing scientific study with the results made known to the public.

Another organization that collects information about UFO sightings is the Aerial Phenomena Research Organization (APRO) with headquarters in Tucson, Arizona. Founded in 1952, it is the oldest of the civilian saucer groups. Like NICAP, APRO claims that some UFOs are of extraterrestrial origin and that information about them is being withheld by the government. APRO has suggested, however, that the Central Intelligence Agency, rather than the Air Force, is responsible for the secrecy.

NICAP and APRO are the largest and best known of the civilian groups devoted to the collection of information about UFOs, but there are many others, both in the United States and in foreign countries. Civilian Saucer Intelligence, Interplanetary Intelligence of Unidentified Flying Objects, World Society of the Flying Saucer, and Borderland Sciences Research Associates are just a few of the groups that have been organized in the United States. Some of the groups publish magazines or newsletters.

Many of the people who join civilian UFO organizations are serious students of the subject. The UFOlogists, as they are called, often have a considerable knowledge of science and they want to find out more about what might be causing UFOs to appear. Others join because they are already convinced that UFOs are spaceships from other planets. Many of these people claim to have seen one or more spaceships and some claim to have made contact with the occupants of the extraterrestrial vehicles. Those who report such contacts are called "contactees" and their reports are referred to as "contact" or "occupant" cases. Some of the UFO groups accept the claims of the contactees, but others do not.

NICAP, for one, discourages such claims because there has never been any reliable evidence to back them up.

A contactee usually tells of observing a spacecraft land, or he comes across one that has already landed. Upon closer examination, he sees one or more figures, all or some of whom leave the spacecraft. If the figures resemble little men, as they often do, they are called humanoids. These visitors from another planet have been described as being dressed in a variety of ways, frequently in spacesuits. And some contactees claim to have actually ridden in an extraterrestrial craft.

According to the contactees' stories, the visitors are friendly. They often express concern about the future of the planet earth and curiosity about the contactee himself. They are able to make themselves understood by speaking in the language of the contactee or by using thought transference.

While the contactee has little trouble understanding a humanoid, he has a great deal of trouble finding a reputable UFO investigator who will believe his story. So far, humanoids have left no evidence behind them to prove that a visit actually took place. However, lack of proof does not discourage the contactees. They continue to tell about their unusual experiences and to write about them, often for a fee.

One man who did this was an amateur astronomer named George Adamski. He claimed that on several occasions during the 1950s he talked with visiting spacemen from other planets using a combination of telepathy and sign language. He also made journeys in the visitors' spacecraft, including a trip around the moon. As proof, Adamski offered a number of photographs whose authenticity was widely questioned. Undaunted, Adamski wrote books and magazine articles about his experiences and gave lectures in the United States and Europe.

Only the true believers in occupant cases have accepted without challenge Adamski's stories about conversations with visitors from other planets and trips in their spaceships. In 1964, however, there was an occupant, or at least a semi-occupant, case that found wide acceptance.

Late in the afternoon of April 24, 1964, Sergeant Lonnie Zamora of the Socorro, New Mexico, police force was on duty in one of the town's patrol cars when he saw a speeder heading south. The speeding car was about three blocks away but Sergeant Zamora began a chase that led him south toward the city limits. He was still about three blocks behind the speeder when, in his words: "I heard a roar and saw a flame in the sky to the southwest, some distance away, possibly a half-mile or a mile." Zamora knew that there was a dynamite shack somewhere in that area. He decided to investigate.

In the report that he made later the police officer said the noise he heard was "a roar, not a blast, not a jet. It changed from high frequency to low frequency and then stopped." He described the flame as "bluish and sort of orange, too." He recalled that it seemed motionless and narrower at the top than at the bottom. He didn't notice if the top was level, or if there was anything above the flame, but Zamora's observations were handicapped by the fact that he was still driving the police car. Moreover, he had left the highway and was heading west into the setting sun on a rough gravel road.

To reach the source of the sound and flame Zamora had to climb a steep, bumpy hill. On his first two attempts he managed to get only halfway to the top. His third try was successful but by then he no longer heard the noise or saw the flame.

From the top of the hill the gravel road continued westward. Zamora was driving slowly, looking for the dynamite shack, when he saw something shiny about 150 or 200 yards to the south. From the road it appeared to be an overturned car, so the police officer stopped. Then he saw what appeared to be two figures in white coveralls, standing close to the shiny object. According to Zamora they were "normal in shape, but possibly they were small adults or large kids." One of them turned to look at the police car and, as Zamora recalled, "seemed startled, seemed to quickly jump somewhat."

After a few seconds the puzzled officer put his car into gear and drove toward the wreck which appeared white "like aluminum." It was oblong in shape. Zamora thought it might be an overturned white car that was standing on its radiator or trunk. As he moved forward he called police headquarters to report that he was going to investigate a possible accident. He was still talking when he brought his car to a halt.

In his haste to leave the car, Zamora dropped his mike. He picked it up and started for the gully where he had seen the white object and the two figures in coveralls. As Zamora told the story, he had taken only a few steps when he heard a loud roar similar to the one he had heard earlier. He saw the blue and orange flame again and this time it was under the object that was rising slowly. There was no smoke, but dust was blowing about in the gully. As the object rose, Zamora noticed that it seemed to have no windows or doors. On its side, he could see what appeared to be an insignia with red lettering.

Startled by the noise and flame and afraid that the object would blow up any minute, Zamora turned and ran. As he did so, he stumbled against his car and dropped his pre-

This is where Sergeant Lonnie Zamora said he saw a UFO that looked like an overturned car and two figures in white coveralls. Some of the brush in the gully near Socorro, New Mexico, was reported to be charred. U.S. Air Force

Investigators used stones to mark the shallow depressions that may have been made by the landing pads of the Socorro UFO.   U.S. Air Force

scription glasses. A high-pitched, whining sound replaced the roar. It lasted about a second and was followed by complete silence. Zamora looked back. He could see the object moving away, traveling 10, or perhaps 15, feet above the ground. Although its speed was considerable, it made no noise and produced no flame.

Shortly after the object disappeared, Sergeant Sam Chavez of the New Mexico State Police joined Zamora. It was while the two men were examining some charred brush in the gully that Chavez noticed four shallow, V-shaped depressions in the gully floor. They were 12 to 14 inches long, one to two inches deep and arranged in a rough diamond shape. Near one of the depressions Chavez found five smaller prints.

Before long the Socorro deputy sheriff, an FBI agent and the Army captain in charge of a nearby tracking station arrived at the gully. The FBI agent took a statement from Officer Zamora and the Army man examined the area and measured distances. Their work and the photographs taken the next morning by Sergeant Chavez became part of the evidence in the Socorro case.

Although radar at Holloman Air Force Base and the White Sands Missile Range, both located near Socorro, did not track an unidentified object on April 24, Officer Zamora's sighting was considered an important one by Project Blue Book and by civilian UFO groups, including NICAP. Zamora was a reliable witness as were the men who examined the area shortly after the sighting. Moreover, the object that Zamora saw could not be identified. If it had been a conventional aircraft or a balloon, he would have recognized it. An investigation revealed that no experimental craft that even roughly resembled the object he saw was in the air near Socorro that day. So in spite of the little men in white whose presence near the UFO would normally have caused many people to view Sergeant Zamora's report with skepticism, the Socorro case was widely accepted as a good "unknown" by civilian UFO groups and by the Air Force as well.

5

The "Thing" and Other Mysteries

One of the most puzzling of all UFO sightings took place near Exeter, New Hampshire, during the early morning hours of September 3, 1965, when a young man named Norman Muscarello and two police officers saw a flying object that has never been adequately explained. Norman, who saw the UFO first, was walking on Route 150 toward his home in Exeter. He had been visiting a friend in Amesbury, Massachusetts, about 12 miles from Exeter. Having no car of his own, he had started home on foot, hoping that a passing motorist would give him a ride. Traffic was light on Route 150, however, and he had walked most of the way. Now it was late, about 2 A.M., and he still had a few miles left to go.

Norman was passing an open field when he saw something that he could hardly believe. Above the field and coming directly toward him was what appeared to be a huge round shape, as big as a house. He later estimated that it was

80 or 90 feet in diameter. There seemed to be a rim of bright, pulsating lights, that cast a red glow, around the center. The weird object appeared to wobble as it moved silently through the air toward the frightened young man. Recovering slightly from his initial shock, Norman realized that he might be hit if he remained where he was. He dove into a shallow ditch that ran along the side of the road.

From the ditch, Muscarello watched the "thing," as he was to call it, move away. Then he scrambled out of the ditch and dashed for the nearest house. There was no help to be had there, however. Norman pounded on the door and called loudly, but no one answered. By now the thing had disappeared completely and Norman wondered what he should do next. As he turned away from the house, he saw the lights of a car coming down the highway. He ran to the road, waving his arms and calling, and the car stopped. Its occupants, a middle-aged couple, agreed to take him to the police station in Exeter.

Although Norman was still frightened when he arrived at the police station, he had already decided to go back to the place where he had seen the thing. He told his story to the policeman manning the desk and asked if an officer could go with him.

At first the policeman listened to Norman with a certain amount of skepticism. A story about an object as big as a house floating through the air sounded like a prank. But the young man was visibly upset and he seemed sincere in his insistence that he had indeed seen something weird. The desk officer agreed to call in a police car.

Eugene Bertrand, the patrolman who answered the call,

had a strange story of his own to tell. About an hour earlier he had seen what he thought might be a stalled car and stopped to investigate. The occupant of the car told him that she had been badly frightened by a large airborne object, with flashing red lights, that followed her car for miles. She had managed to keep a few feet ahead of it but once the object left, she had stopped to calm her shattered nerves. Patrolman Bertrand had not made a special report because he thought the woman had just imagined something was following her. When Norman heard Bertrand's story, he said: "It sounds exactly like what I saw."

It was about 3 A.M. when Norman and Officer Bertrand reached the open field where Norman had encountered the thing. From the highway they saw nothing unusual: a few houses and other buildings and some trees in the distance. It was a clear moonlight night and visibility was excellent. They decided to walk across the field.

Officer Bertrand had just about made up his mind that the UFO had been a helicopter. He was discussing his theory with Norman when horses in a nearby corral began to kick and whinny. At almost the same moment Norman shouted: "I see it! I see it!" What seemed to be a large round shape, banded with bright red lights, was slowly rising behind the trees. Without making a sound, it advanced toward them with a wobbling motion.

Pulling Norman behind him, Bertrand ran for his patrol car. Once they were safely inside, he called the Exeter police station. "I've seen it myself!" he shouted into the mike.

For several minutes the two men watched the object as it appeared to hover about 100 feet above the ground, still wobbling and absolutely silent. Its pulsating lights cast an eerie red glow over everything. Because the lights were so bright, the men had trouble making out the object's shape, even though it was barely the length of a football field away.

Soundlessly the UFO began to move away. As it did so, another police car pulled up. Its occupant, Patrolman David Hunt, had heard Bertrand's call to the Exeter police station. With Muscarello and Bertrand, Hunt watched the object disappear behind some trees. It seemed to be traveling in the direction of the ocean. Hunt observed the same pulsating red lights and wobbling motion that Patrolman Bertrand and Norman Muscarello had seen previously.

In the report that they made later at the police station, the men described the lights as bright red and round and about the size of a baseball. There were five of them, arranged fairly close together in a row. The entire row was tilted at a 60-degree angle to the horizon, that never seemed to vary. The lights flashed in sequence along the row and then back again. And they were bright enough to illuminate the entire landscape with a red glow. When the object descended to a lower altitude, which it did from time to time while Muscarello and Bertrand—and later Hunt—watched, the movement resembled a falling leaf.

Because busy Pease Air Force Base was only a few miles from Exeter, the three men were used to seeing airplanes flying at night. In addition, Bertrand was an Air Force veteran. They agreed that what they had seen was definitely not a B-52, a B-47, a jet fighter, a helicopter or anything else known to be at Pease. They conceded that it might be some new secret craft. But it seemed unlikely that the Air Force would allow a low-level test flight so close to a populated area.

Still puzzling over what they had seen, Norman, Bertrand and Hunt returned to Exeter where Norman's worried mother was waiting for him. The young man was still obviously shaken by what he had seen. His mother described him as "white as a ghost."

Following its standard procedure in UFO cases, the Exeter police department notified Pease Air Force Base of the sighting. The next afternoon two Air Force officers arrived in Exeter to interview Patrolmen Bertrand and Hunt and Norman Muscarello. During the investigation, which extended over several days, the Air Force also looked into the sighting on the same night of a similar-appearing UFO at Hampton, a town not far from Exeter.

As soon as news of the mysterious sightings began to circulate in the Exeter area, a number of people announced that they, too, had seen a UFO, perhaps the same one. They usually explained that they hadn't reported it earlier because they weren't sure of what they did see, or they were afraid people would laugh at their story. Saucer-watching became a popular evening pastime and during the next few weeks there were more sightings, including another one by Norman Muscarello.

Norman, who had joined the Navy, decided that he would try to see the thing again before he left Exeter to report to the Great Lakes Naval Training Center. Almost every night he and some friends visited the field on Route 150 where the thing had appeared on September 3. Their watch was unsuccessful until they decided to keep an all-night vigil. The sun was just coming up when they saw what they described as a saucer-shaped object in the sky. Unlike the UFO that Norman had seen on September 3, this one had a bluish color that resembled metal.

Another sighting was reported by a high school senior named Ron Smith, his mother and his aunt who encountered a UFO when they were driving near Exeter on a warm, clear night in late September. They described what they saw as a large, oval-shaped object with a bright red light near its top. A glowing white light illuminated the bottom. The UFO came spinning out of the sky, passed over Smith's car and stopped. Then it passed over the car a second and third time before moving away.

A frightened Ron had driven his equally frightened passengers into Exeter before he decided that they should probably go back for another look in case they had just been imagining things. When they returned, they found the UFO in approximately the same place. This time it passed over the car once and disappeared for good. Now convinced beyond any doubt that they had really seen something odd, Ron and his passengers drove to the Exeter police station to make a report. Like Norman Muscarello and the two patrolmen, they couldn't identify what they had seen, but they knew it wasn't an airplane or a helicopter.

Still another sighting in the Exeter area was made by a woman who reported that she saw a large, red blinking light in the night sky. It moved rapidly toward her from the southeast, stopped suddenly and moved off in a slightly different direction. The object appeared to have a cone shape, but the brightness of the red light made it difficult to see clearly.

While she was uncertain of the exact shape, the observer knew she wasn't looking at an airplane. The way the object moved and the way it stopped in midair convinced her of that.

There were daylight sightings, too, one of them by a woman who reported seeing a wingless, metal-colored UFO when she was driving near Exeter. This UFO was able to reverse direction and make abrupt changes in speed. It had no lights and was completely silent. The observer watched the UFO from as close as 200 or 300 feet. Although she saw it for no more than two minutes at the most, she was absolutely convinced that the flying object was neither an airplane nor a helicopter.

These were only a few of the many sightings reported from the Exeter area during the fall of 1965. Such a large number of UFO reports coming from one place in a short period of time constituted a UFO flap and this one attracted nationwide attention. Among those who became interested in the Exeter UFOs was a writer named John Fuller. He decided to write an article about them.

Fuller went to Exeter and talked with more than sixty people who claimed to have seen UFOs. He also talked with members of the Exeter police department and officials at Pease Air Force Base. His article appeared in the February 8, 1966, issue of *Look* magazine and in the *Reader's Digest* for May, 1966. Then he gathered more material about UFOs and wrote a book which he called *Incident at Exeter*. Much of the information in this chapter about the UFOs seen by Norman Muscarello and other residents of the Exeter area is from Fuller's account.

During his research in Exeter, Fuller was impressed with the sincerity of most of the people who had seen UFOs. They appeared to be intelligent and reliable citizens who would not make false reports. Moreover, their reports were remarkably similar, even though the sightings were made at different times and places.

When he began his investigation, John Fuller was, in his own words, "a friendly skeptic" on the subject of UFOs. But after his interviews and other research, he came to the conclusion that the objects seen at Exeter were true UFOs. He also concluded that interplanetary spaceships under intelligent control provided the best explanation of the Exeter UFOs.

On October 27, 1965, the Air Force announced the results of its investigation of the UFO seen at Exeter during the early morning hours of September 3. There were two possible explanations, the Air Force said. The Strategic Air Command had conducted a high-altitude exercise called "Big Beast" in the Exeter area that night and, in addition, there were five B-47 jets in the air. Therefore, Norman Muscarello, Patrolman Eugene Bertrand and Patrolman David Hunt might have seen an airplane that they mistook for a UFO. Or they may have been confused by stars and planets that appeared to twinkle more than normal and to move in "unusual formations" due to a temperature inversion in the Exeter area that night. However, the sighting was officially classified as "Unidentified" because these were only possible, not proven, explanations. No one knows for sure what Muscarello, Bertrand and Hunt saw on September 3. Most of the other Exeter sightings are also unexplained.

On the night of August 30, 1965, three Urbana, Ohio, high school students had an experience they will never forget. The boys, Mike Lilly, Nelson Smith and Thomas Nastoff, were driving down a road near the local fairgrounds when they saw what appeared to be a ball of light coming down from the sky. It seemed to hit the road directly in front of the car in which the boys were riding before it bounced back into the air. Mike, who was driving, slammed on the brakes. "I think we might have hit it if I hadn't stopped," he said later.

The three frightened boys decided to leave before the ball came back. As they sped away, they saw it again. This time it was about 100 feet above the ground, heading south. Behind it trailed a streak of light perhaps 2 feet long.

Although the mysterious ball apparently remained in view for no more than a few seconds, there were only minor variations in the boys' reports of what they had seen. Mike, for example, described a round ball, "about the same color as a star, only brighter," while Nelson thought the UFO had more of a disc shape. The boys estimated that the object was between five and eight feet in diameter. They saw no wings or other projections and heard no sound. Although the object itself was very bright, it did not not appear to give off any light and it did not change color. One of the boys reported that the UFO was traveling "sort of fast, but not too fast." Another suggested that it might have been traveling as fast as an airplane.

When they made their report to the county sheriff, the boys were unable to suggest any explanation for what they had seen. Its identity remains a mystery.

61

In 1966, residents of northwestern New Jersey were puzzled by a number of sightings near Wanaque Reservoir, a large water-storage area. The series of sightings began shortly after six o'clock on the evening of January 11. A newspaper editor named Howard Ball was driving to his office in Paterson when he saw an extremely bright light in the sky. He later described it as a "brilliant blue-white-type light." It was a steady, rather than flashing or pulsating, light and was moving in a generally northwest direction toward Wanaque Reservoir.

In order to observe the strange light a little longer, the newspaperman pulled his car over to the side of the road and stopped. Before resuming his trip to Paterson, Ball watched the light make one 90° turn and then another, pausing briefly before each change of direction.

That night the newspaper received word that a number of residents of the Wanaque area had reported seeing UFOs. Curious about what he himself had seen and wondering if the Wanaque reports were about the same thing, Ball decided to do a little investigating. He called the nearest air base, which was McGuire Air Force Base near Trenton, New Jersey. Had either planes or helicopters from McGuire flown over the Wanaque area that evening? The answer was no. When Editor Ball explained the reason for his question, he was referred to Stewart Air Force Base at Newburgh, New York. But Stewart had no aircraft in the area, either.

Thinking that a helicopter with a strong light was the most logical explanation of what he had seen, the editor continued his investigation with more telephone calls. The New Jersey State Police had no helicopter in the air at the time of the sightings. Neither did any of the radio stations that used traffic helicopters. Finally, Ball had to give up. He could find no explanation for the bright light that he had observed moving across the sky.

Among the others who saw unusual lights in the sky that night were the mayor of Wanaque Borough, the mayor's fourteen-year-old son and two borough councilmen. One of the councilmen had received reports of a strange object in the sky above the reservoir and had alerted the mayor.

When the mayor and his companions arrived at the reservoir, they saw a light "a little bigger than a star" that changed its color from green to red to white. During the four or five minutes that they watched it, the light moved only slightly, if at all, but it disappeared completely while they were moving their car to get more protection from the cold wind.

Two hours later the chief of the Reservoir Police Force and one of his officers observed an extremely bright light above the reservoir. They compared it to the beam from the headlight of a locomotive and noted that looking at it hurt their eyes. The light appeared to be stationary and made no sound. This time it remained above the reservoir for almost an hour.

More unexplained lights were observed above the reservoir during the ensuing months, but the strangest sighting of all took place that fall. Shortly after 9 P.M. on October 11, Sergeant Ben Thompson of the Reservoir Police Force was on duty in his patrol car when he received a call from Pompton Lakes, a town near the reservoir. The Pompton Lakes police had received a report of a UFO that seemed to be heading

63

for the reservoir. They told Sergeant Thompson where it might be. Would he drive over there and take a look around?

Thompson set off at once and within five minutes he had spotted a bright light in the sky. When he first saw it, the light appeared to be stationary, but as he watched from about 250 feet away, it began to move rapidly in a series of square turns. The light was very bright and, Thompson recalled later, it seemed to be about the size of a car, perhaps 8 feet in diameter. In spite of its rapid movement, it made no sound.

As the light maneuvered at an altitude that he estimated to be about 250 feet, Sergeant Thompson made out a vague shape. From one direction the object seemed to be a revolving, brightly lit ball with a dome protruding from the top. At other times, it looked like a disc. However, the object was too bright for Thompson to make sure of its shape. It was so bright that when it disappeared he could see nothing at all; he was temporarily blinded. Sergeant Thompson had watched the mysterious light for about three minutes when it moved in the direction of some hills and vanished.

Among the explanations that have been suggested for the strange lights seen over Wanaque Reservoir are airplanes, helicopters, bright planets, automobile lights reflected by a temperature inversion and electrical discharges in the atmosphere. Which of the suggested explanations is correct, if indeed one of them is, remains a mystery.

6

Hoaxes, Deceptions and Delusions

For one reason or another, there are people who claim to have seen unidentified flying objects when they know their claims are false. Sometimes the bogus claims are intended as a joke. Other false claimants hope to make money by selling their stories or photographs to newspapers and magazines. The desire for fame, or at least attention, has been responsible for a number of false claims about UFOs. Some reports result from the delusions of unstable persons. Fortunately, false claims about UFO sightings are relatively easy to identify because they don't hold up under investigation. Occasionally, however, the fabrications receive a great deal of publicity before they are exposed.

One widely publicized UFO hoax took place in 1947 not long after Kenneth Arnold announced that he had seen nine mysterious flying discs near Mount Rainier. The hoaxers also

Two eleven-year-old boys found this object which supposedly fell to the earth with a whooshing sound. Upon investigation, it proved to be not material from a spaceship, but plastic residue from a local factory. U.S. Air Force

claimed to have seen disclike flying objects and they concocted an elaborate story to back up their claims.

What came to be known as the Maury Island mystery began late in June 1947 when two men, who identified themselves as harbor patrolmen, reported seeing six flying objects near Maury Island in Puget Sound, about three miles from Tacoma, Washington.

According to the patrolmen's story, it was a gray day with low-hanging clouds. Their patrol near Maury Island had been uneventful until six silver-colored, doughnut-shaped objects appeared just beneath the clouds and began moving in the direction of the patrol boat. The UFOs were no more than 500 feet away when they stopped, close enough for the two patrolmen to get a good look at them. What the patrolmen saw was six flat, circular objects, each about 100 feet in diameter with a 25-foot hole in the center. The UFOs had what appeared to be large portholes around their edges.

As the men watched, five of the UFOs circled the sixth which appeared to be in trouble. Then one of the circling UFOs seemed to join up with the disabled craft. When they separated after a few minutes, the patrolmen heard a thud; until then the UFOs had been absolutely silent. At that moment, sheets of what appeared to be light metal fell from the disabled UFO. They were followed by a hard substance resembling rock. Some of the rocklike material landed on the boat, damaging it and killing a dog on board.

As soon as the rock shower subsided, the patrolmen headed for a beach on Maury Island where some of the material from the UFO had landed. The boat had almost reached the beach when the UFOs sped off. The patrolmen had already taken photographs of the UFOs, however, and now they gathered up several chunks of the rock as further proof of what they had seen.

Before they left the island the two patrolmen tried to call their headquarters, but they were unable to use their radio. At this point they returned to Tacoma.

When the photographs of the UFOs were developed, they

showed the six doughnut-shaped objects but the pictures were badly fogged, perhaps by some kind of radiation. Before they could show the photographs to anyone, however, the patrolmen received a visit from a mysterious stranger who told them to forget what had happened near Maury Island.

This was the story that the hoaxers sent to a magazine publisher in Chicago along with some samples of the material they claimed had fallen from the disabled UFO. The publisher was interested in the story for his magazine but he wanted more information. To get it, he hired Kenneth Arnold, a man who was an authority on flying discs because he had seen nine of them.

Arnold flew to Tacoma where he had several puzzling interviews with the two patrolmen who seemed evasive. Furthermore, they changed their story from time to time and they failed to produce the photographs they claimed to have taken. And to Arnold's dismay, Tacoma newspapers printed accounts of the interviews which were supposed to be secret.

Finally, the bewildered Arnold called on the Air Force for help and two intelligence officers were dispatched to Tacoma. They talked with Arnold and interviewed the two harbor patrolmen. They also checked on some of the "facts" in the patrolmen's story.

When their investigation was completed, the two officers reported their findings to intelligence officials at McChord Air Force Base, near Tacoma. Then they took off in a B-25 for their home base. Unfortunately, the B-25 crashed a few hours later, killing both men.

Although the cause of the crash was traced to a burning

exhaust stack that set one of the plane's wings on fire, rumors about hostile spaceships persisted. In one popular version of the crash, the B-25 was carrying samples of the material found on Maury Island and someone or something wanted the samples destroyed before they could be analyzed.

The Maury Island mystery turned out to be not a mystery but a hoax. The Air Force investigators had discovered that the "harbor patrolmen" owned an old boat and made their living salvaging floating lumber from Puget Sound. There were no photographs and there was no mysterious stranger. The rocklike material found on Maury Island was actually slag from a smelter plant.

When they concocted their story, the hoaxers had planned to sell it to a magazine. The arrival of Kenneth Arnold and, later, of the Air Force investigators had dashed that hope. The crash of the B-25 brought the Maury Island hoax to an unplanned and unfortunate end.

Unlike the Maury Island mystery, some hoaxes have worked out just as they were planned. One of these "successful" hoaxes took place in Westport, Connecticut, in 1966 when a group of boys set out to prove that many UFO reports are inaccurate. To carry out their hoax they purchased a number of weather balloons from a surplus supply house. From time to time they launched one of their balloons with a lighted red flare hanging beneath it. The balloon carried the pulsating red light on an erratic journey across the sky until eventually the light disappeared.

After each landing the boys checked Westport area newspapers for UFO reports. Some observers reported seeing a blinking red light; some saw a cluster of red lights. An oval object with raylike spokes, a cluster of multicolored lights, and a UFO with a searchlight trained on the ground were also reported. There were even rumors that the National Aeronautics and Space Administration had investigated the Westport UFOs and refused to reveal the result.

Finally, this hoax, too, was uncovered, but the boys had demonstrated that UFO observations can be unreliable. Their experiment worked almost too well. When newspapers carried accounts of the hoax, some of the "UFO observers" refused to believe that they had seen a weather balloon carrying a red flare. It was an authentic UFO, they insisted.

In the fall of 1967 many residents of Alamosa, Colorado, were convinced that a pet horse named Snippy had been mysteriously killed by the occupants of a UFO. Snippy belonged to a family named Lewis who boarded her at the Harry King ranch. The Lewises and the Kings were related.

One night, Snippy failed to show up at the ranch house for her usual drink of water. When another day passed with no sign of Snippy, the ranch owner became concerned. On the third day he went looking for Snippy and found her. But the horse was dead and there were several unusual things about the carcass.

Snippy's head and neck had been completely skinned. The bleached head and neck bones were still attached to the rest of the body, however. There was no sign of blood although the horse had a deep cut just above the shoulder.

The next day an examination of the area by the dead horse's owners and the rancher revealed a number of slight depressions in the ground. Some of the depressions were discolored and might have been exhaust marks. A bush about

100 yards from the carcass had been flattened. The investigators detected a "medicinal, incenselike odor" near the horse and they noted that the exposed head and neck bones had turned pink. When Mrs. Lewis touched a piece of horseflesh, her hand turned pink and burned until she washed it. The same thing happened when she touched a piece of metal covered with horsehair.

Before and after Snippy's mysterious death a number of UFOs were sighted in the Alamosa area. Only a few weeks earlier a couple had reported seeing two UFOs that were outlined with a dull glow. At first the UFOs were some distance apart but they had moved closer together and hovered for several minutes. They had then descended to the ground and seemed to merge with the vegetation.

An Alamosa service station attendant was driving his car when he saw an object that looked like a box kite fly across the highway ahead of him. The UFO made no sound. Thinking it might be some unusual kind of aircraft, he drove to the airport for a closer look in case the strange craft landed. On the way he lost sight of the UFO, which did not land at the airport.

Snippy's owners were among those who saw UFOs near Alamosa. They reported seeing three pulsating red and green lights that moved in a southwesterly direction. After the lights had been in view for five minutes or more, the third light exploded with a yellow flash followed by a second flash and a puff of smoke. They saw fragments falling to the ground after the second explosion. A farmer also reported seeing an explosion that night.

The story of Snippy's mysterious death made the front

71

pages of newspapers all over the United States, along with accounts of the many UFOs that had been sighted in the Alamosa area. Many readers suspected that the UFOs were somehow connected with Snippy's death. The Lewises thought so, too, and they arranged to have Snippy's pasture checked with a Geiger counter. If a spaceship had landed there, the radiation level might be high. The man who conducted the test reported that the radiation reading did appear to be higher than normal.

As a result of the newspaper stories, various organizations and individuals become interested in the strange death of Snippy, the horse. NICAP, the civilian UFO organization, sent four investigators to Alamosa. They interviewed the Lewis and King families, took pictures and collected soil samples and other evidence that might help prove or disprove the theory that a UFO was involved in Snippy's death. APRO also sent one of its investigators to Alamosa.

A Denver pathologist and blood specialist who wished to remain anonymous volunteered to examine the carcass. He expressed surprise when he found that Snippy's brain cavity and the center of her spinal column were empty.

Speculation about what had happened to Snippy increased when another horse was found dead not far from the King ranch. It developed that the horse had been shot, but later four more horses and four cows died mysteriously. During this period there were many reports of UFO sightings in the Alamosa area.

While the flying saucer theory was the most popular explanation of Snippy's death, there were other theories as well. One was that the whole thing was a very elaborate hoax designed to make people think that the sinister occupants of a UFO were involved. According to this theory, which was explained in an article in the *Denver Post,* Snippy was immobilized with a tranquilizer pellet shot from a gun. Then the hoaxers suspended the horse from a pole rig and placed her head in an acid bath to dissolve everything but the bones. This would account for the empty brain cavity and some of the depressions found in the ground near the dead horse. Acid would also have produced the exhaustlike marks and caused Mrs. Lewis' hand to burn when she touched the horseflesh and the piece of metal. Unfortunately, there was no proof for any part of the hoax theory.

At the time of Snippy's death, the University of Colorado was conducting a special study of UFOs for the Air Force. (We will learn more about the special study later.) Because of the large number of UFO reports coming from the Alamosa area and the widely held belief that the UFOs had something to do with the horse's death, the Colorado Project sent its investigators to Alamosa along with the chief of surgery of Colorado State University's College of Veterinary Medicine and Biomedical Sciences. The veterinary expert examined Snippy's carcass and found that the horse had died of natural causes, probably a severe infection in the right flank and leg. Such an infection would kill a horse very quickly. The veterinarian theorized that the deep shoulder cut that had seemed so mysterious was probably the result of an act of kindness on the part of somebody who found the dying horse and stabbed her to end her misery. Magpies and coyotes had then found the carcass which explained the empty body cavities.

The Colorado investigators accepted the veterinarian's explanation. Moreover, they found no evidence of radiation or exhaust marks or anything else to connect Snippy's death with UFOs or UFO occupants, real or imagined.

After its own investigation, NICAP came to the same conclusion. APRO, however, thought that Snippy's strange death merited further study.

Since none of the groups and individuals who investigated Snippy's death found evidence that UFOs were involved in any way, it wasn't a UFO case at all. But the case of Snippy, the horse, is a good example of how wild rumors and speculative stories in the newspapers can produce a UFO flap.

In 1953 a dead monkey was involved in a UFO hoax. The hoaxers were three young men who lived in Atlanta, Georgia. One night they brought a strange-looking creature to the editorial offices of the *Atlanta Constitution*. The trio told newsmen that they had just driven up a hill and reached the top when they saw a strange, red saucer-shaped object on the road ahead. Three figures that resembled small humans were running toward the object. The driver slammed on his brakes but before the car stopped, it hit one of the creatures. The other two entered the UFO which turned from its original red color to blue and sped away. The young men had then driven to the *Constitution* offices, bringing the dead creature with them.

When the story appeared in the *Constitution*, it created a sensation. Hundreds of people wanted to see the little man from another planet. The hoaxers received requests for pictures and information from all over the country. They also received a visit from two representatives of Project Blue Book.

In the course of the investigation that followed, the "little man from another planet" was quickly identified as a monkey whose fur had been shaved.. The monkey's tail had been cut off as well.

At first the hoaxers insisted that their story was true. Finally, however, one of them admitted that he had planned the whole thing to win a ten-dollar bet with a friend. He had bet that he could get his name and picture printed in a newspaper and inventing a little man from another planet had seemed like a good way to do it. The hoaxer won the ten dollars but after a police investigation he was fined *forty* dollars.

A Florida scoutmaster was responsible for an elaborate UFO hoax. He prepared for it by offering to give four of his scouts a ride home after their evening scout meeting. The date was August 19, 1952.

One of the boys had been dropped off at his home and the scoutmaster was driving down a back road toward a second boy's home when he saw lights that flickered briefly behind some scrub pines bordering the road. He mentioned the lights to the boys but they had not noticed anything. When the lights reappeared, however, the boys did see them. The scoutmaster stopped his car and they discussed what the lights might be, mentioning flying saucers, among other things.

They had driven a short distance down the road when the scoutmaster stopped again. "If the lights belong to an airplane that has crashed in the woods, someone might need help," the scoutmaster told the boys. They agreed, and turning his car around, the scoutmaster drove back to the place where they had seen the lights.

Leaving the boys in the car with instructions to go for help if he didn't return in fifteen minutes, the scoutmaster set off through the woods. He was carrying two flashlights and a machete.

As the scoutmaster told the story later, he had traveled about 50 yards when he noticed a "sharp" or "pungent" odor. He also felt the air around him getting warmer. Using the north star as a guide, he made his way through thick palmetto undergrowth until he came to a clearing.

Both the odor and the heat were more noticeable in the clearing. He found it difficult to breathe and he began to feel that someone was watching him. At this point the scoutmaster looked up to check the position of the north star and discovered that he couldn't see the sky at all because a large, dark shape was hovering about 30 feet above his head.

The scoutmaster recalled that he was too frightened to move at first, but he finally backed away from the object. As he moved away, the air became cooler and he felt better. He even managed to shine his flashlight at the object. He saw that it was saucer-shaped with a smooth, dark-gray surface and a bottom that was slightly concave and seemed to glow. There was a dome, like a turret, in the middle of the upper part. Around the object's edge he noticed a series of vanes about a foot apart. Small openings, or nozzles, were spaced between the vanes.

While the scoutmaster stood looking up at the mysterious

object, he heard a sound like a door opening. Then a small ball of red fire began to move toward him from the side of the UFO. He covered his face with his hands as a red mist surrounded him. Then he fainted.

Meanwhile, the three boys had watched the beam of the scoutmaster's flashlight move through the woods. They saw him shine the light ahead before he entered the clearing. A minute or so later, they saw him shine the light into the air. Then they saw a ball of red fire move toward the light.

When the scouts saw the ball of fire, they jumped from the car and ran to the nearest farmhouse. The breathless, excited boys told a jumbled story about seeing lights and balls of red fire but the farmer finally understood that their scoutmaster was in trouble down the road. He called the Florida State Highway Patrol, who notified the county sheriff. Within a few minutes a deputy sheriff and a constable had arrived at the farmhouse to take the boys back to the place where they had last seen their scoutmaster.

The deputy's car had just pulled up near the scoutmaster's car when the scoutmaster himself ran out of the woods. He seemed to be badly frightened. The hair on his arms was singed and there were burn holes in his cap.

Accompanied by the two police officers, the scoutmaster went back into the woods. When they reached the clearing they found the machete and the still-burning flashlight where the scoutmaster had dropped them. However, there was no trace of the second flashlight that he had carried in his pocket. After a thorough search, they marked the place in the clearing where the grass seemed to be flattened and left.

Later that night the deputy sheriff reported the incident

to the Air Force. The case seemed important enough to merit an immediate investigation and Project Blue Book sent two representatives to Florida the next day.

When Project Blue Book's investigators interviewed the scoutmaster, he appeared to be telling the truth about his harrowing experience. Moreover, the three boys backed up the story. The Air Force doctor who examined the scoutmaster wasn't entirely convinced, however. He pointed out that the scoutmaster could have burned his arms with a cigarette lighter or with matches. And he suggested that it might be a good idea to check the scoutmaster's claim that he had served in the Marines during World War II.

In addition to interviewing the scoutmaster and the three boys, the Project Blue Book investigators examined the clearing in the woods. They found no burned matches or evidence that fireworks or flares had been lighted there. In fact, they found nothing at all to contradict the scoutmaster's story.

The investigation was almost completed and the Blue Book men were getting ready to leave when the first suspicious evidence turned up. The investigators learned that the scoutmaster had been a Marine, but only briefly; he had been discharged for being absent without leave and stealing a car. Then the scoutmaster was quoted in a Palm Beach newspaper as saying that he had identified what he had seen in the woods, but if he told anyone it would create a national panic. Nevertheless, he hired a press agent to help sell his story.

Evidence of a hoax mounted when tests by the Federal

Bureau of Investigation indicated that a cigarette had burned holes in the scoutmaster's cap.

When the three scouts were questioned again, they were no longer positive about what they had seen. The scouts had no part in the hoax, however. They had merely accepted the scoutmaster's story for which he had prepared them by talking about flying saucers. The lights flickering in the woods had been real enough. They belonged to planes landing at a nearby airport. But everything else in the scoutmaster's story was exposed as a hoax, an unsuccessful hoax.

Photographic material often figures in UFO hoaxes. Still photos of UFOs are especially easy to fake. The photographer may use a model of some kind which he photographs and claims is a UFO, or he may produce a UFO-like image from a double exposure or by retouching a negative. Because they are so easy to fake, photos presented as proof of a UFO sighting will be studied carefully. The person who took them will be investigated as well because a UFO photograph is only as reliable as the person who took it.

Analysis of UFO photos is often made more difficult by the absence of the original negatives which forces the investigators to work with prints or negatives made from prints. In recent years many UFO photos have been taken with Polaroid cameras which produce only prints. Nevertheless, experts can identify most UFO hoaxes based on false photographic evidence.

Sometimes, however, even the experts are stumped. This happens when the person who took the photographs appears to be reliable and his photographs authentic, but enough inconsistencies exist to at least raise the question of fabrication. One such case was reported from California in 1965.

On August 3, about noon, a highway traffic engineer was driving near the Santa Ana freeway when he saw something that he described as looking like a large straw hat flying through the air. He estimated that it was about 30 feet in diameter, 150 feet high and 750 feet from his car. The object had a silver, or metallic, color and it made no noise. The engineer stopped his truck, reached for his Polaroid camera and quickly took three pictures, the first through the truck's windshield and two more through the right-door window. At this point he thought he heard a car approaching from the rear and looked back to see if there was enough room for it to pass. When he turned around again the UFO had disappeared, but it had left a ring of smokelike vapor behind. He drove about a mile down the road and took a fourth picture of the vapor.

One of the puzzles about this case was that the traffic engineer did not report his strange experience to anyone. Instead, he finished his day's work and returned to the office. Then he showed the three pictures of the UFO itself to his coworkers. He left the picture that showed the vapor ring in his car and rarely mentioned it in the weeks that followed.

During the next few days several copies were made of the three UFO photos and a set was sent to *Life* magazine. *Life* decided not to use the photos, but on September 20 they appeared in the *Santa Ana Register* and the story was picked up by many other newspapers.

Meanwhile, an investigator from the El Toro Marine Air Station, near Santa Ana, interviewed the engineer and bor-

A UFO that resembled a flying straw hat was photographed in Santa Ana, California, in 1965. After an investigation, Project Blue Book concluded that the Santa Ana UFO photos were a hoax. UPI

rowed the original Polaroid prints which he returned a few days later. Then another puzzling thing happened. According to the engineer, a few hours after the Marine Corps investigator returned the prints, a man in civilian clothing who said he was from the North American Air Defense Command (NORAD) borrowed them. Oddly enough, the engineer gave up his original prints without getting the man's name

81

or asking for a signed receipt. As a result, when an Air Force UFO investigator entered the case the next day, the original prints were not available for study. NORAD has no responsibility for UFO investigations and has denied ever sending a representative to borrow the prints, which have never been located.

Project Blue Book obtained prints made from negatives of the original prints for its investigation of the Santa Ana UFO sighting. After studying the prints, Blue Book photo analysts determined that the flying straw hat was no more than a few feet in diameter, certainly not 30 feet, and no more than 15 or 20 feet above the ground, which was the approximate distance at which the camera had been focused. They arrived at that conclusion because the background in the photos was blurred, while the object and the center stripe on the road were in sharp focus. The analysts used the width of the road to estimate both the size of the object and its elevation.

To further investigate the possibility of a hoax, the Blue Book photo analysts tossed a nine-inch vaporizing tray into the air and photographed it from a distance of 15 to 20 feet. The resulting photos showed a striking resemblance to the engineer's UFO.

When all the evidence had been studied, Project Blue Book concluded that the Santa Ana UFO photos were a hoax.

While Project Blue Book's investigation was under way, NICAP was conducting an intensive investigation of its own. NICAP could find no evidence of a hoax and it called the Air Force conclusion "an insult to the intelligence of the public."

Somewhat later, the Colorado Project reviewed the evidence in the Santa Ana case and found too many discrepancies in the engineer's account of the sighting and in the photographs themselves to make further investigation worthwhile.

Two UFO photos taken in Pennsylvania only a few days after the ones at Santa Ana appear to be authentic but in this case, too, an element of doubt remains. The photographer was seventeen-year-old James Lucci, who, with his twenty-year-old brother, had set up a camera in the driveway of his home to make time exposures of the moon. Two other boys were also present.

James was busy with the camera when what appeared to be a bright, round object suddenly came into view from behind some trees. All of the boys saw it. Realizing that the camera was aimed directly at the object, James quickly closed the shutter. He had time to advance the film and make a second exposure before the UFO rose at high speed and disappeared. The brothers later described the object as a "big, disc-shaped light." It moved quickly into view, hovered for a few seconds, drifted to the right of the moon, hovered again and then climbed out of sight. They described its color as white and they had it in view for about thirty seconds.

Although he had only two exposures on his roll of film, James developed them at once instead of waiting to finish the roll. Both photos showed a bright, saucer-shaped object. In the second exposure the UFO had moved to the right of the moon.

At the suggestion of a friend, James Lucci took the roll of film with the two exposed frames to the *Beaver County*

Times. The editor was interested in Lucci's story but declined to print it or the pictures until their authenticity was established. After a reporter and two photographers had investigated the incident for several days, the *Times* used both the story and the pictures. Its photographers had examined the two negatives and found them to be genuine. A NICAP investigator also analyzed the Lucci negatives and found no evidence of a hoax.

Project Blue Book did not investigate the Lucci sighting, but the Colorado Project reviewed the case a few years later. In the course of their research the Project's photo experts produced pictures similar to the ones taken by James Lucci by photographing a dish held by a short handle and illuminated by a flashlight. The Project's investigators concluded: "The photographs have little value in establishing an extraordinary phenomenon."

The Colorado Project did not claim that the Lucci sighting was a hoax, however. If it was a hoax, it was a clever one and one of the few that has not been exposed rather quickly by UFO investigators.

7

Identified Flying Objects

No one denies that unidentified flying objects exist. The mere fact that an individual reports that he has seen something in the sky that he cannot identify, creates a UFO. But it remains a UFO only as long as it cannot be explained. Most unidentified flying objects eventually become identified flying objects. It follows from this that in many cases there would have been no UFO report and no UFO if the observer had been more knowledgeable about the characteristics of the airplane, the bright planet, or whatever it was that puzzled him when he saw it in the sky.

In 1959 a night aerial refueling operation produced a famous UFO report. It came from Captain Peter W. Killian, the pilot of an American Airlines plane traveling from Newark, New Jersey, to Detroit, Michigan. Killian's plane was over Pennsylvania at an altitude of 8,500 feet, above scattered clouds, when he noticed three bright lights on his left. At first he thought he was seeing part of the constellation Orion but then he saw the real Orion higher in the sky. Moreover, the strange lights, which were yellowish-white in color, varied in intensity and sometimes disappeared completely for short periods. To add to the mystery, the lights seemed to be moving about in the sky.

More than half-convinced that the strange lights were flying saucers, Captain Killian pointed them out to his co-pilot. Then he switched on the intercom and told his passengers that they would see something unusual if they looked out the window on the left. He also contacted two other planes in the area, whose pilots had also seen the lights, and Air Traffic Control in Detroit.

During the forty minutes that the lights remained in view, they were too bright for Killian to make out any shape behind them and he could not tell how far away they were. He was not sure of their speed, either, but they seemed to move more slowly than a jet airplane would.

The story of the strange lights made headlines in the *Detroit Times* which called them "mystery discs." When Killian's return flight reached New York, reporters and photographers were waiting for him and more stories about the mysterious flying lights appeared.

In the meantime, Captain Killian had reported his unusual experience to American Airlines, and the airline had notified the Air Force. Project Blue Book began an investigation. Because of the many stories that had appeared in the press about the flying lights, the Killian case proved a difficult one to handle. There were urgent requests for an explanation from reporters and others before all the facts could be collected and analyzed.

Finally, an Air Force spokesman announced, as a tentative theory, that the lights might have been part of the constellation Orion. Captain Killian immediately rejected this explanation and pointed out that he had seen both the lights and the real Orion that night. Flying saucer fans also rejected the Orion theory. They suspected that the lights were spaceships and Captain Killian was inclined to agree with them.

"I am sure there are people on other planets and that they have solved the problem of space travel," he stated in an interview.

While the controversy raged, the Blue Book investigation continued. Twenty days after the sighting the Air Force made another announcement and this time its explanation of the Killian sighting was no longer tentative. The pilot had seen the lights of a Strategic Air Command KC-97 tanker that was engaged in a night refueling exercise with B-47 bombers at the time and place of the sighting. The KC-97 had several groups of lights that might have looked like one or more lights from a distance and its speed would have been low during the refueling operation. Also, refueling required about forty minutes, the time that the lights remained in view.

In his report to American Airlines, Captain Killian indicated that he had never seen refueling operations at night and knew nothing about an aerial tanker's lights. If he had been familiar with night refueling, there would have been no UFO report and no Killian case in Project Blue Book's files.

In 1951 the Lubbock lights were unidentified flying objects for several weeks. The case began on a hot August night when a geology professor was sitting in his yard with some friends who also were science professors. They were discussing meteors and hoping to see one since meteors were more frequent than usual at that time of the year. As they casually watched the sky the men were startled to see a formation of 15 to 20 yellowish or white lights pass overhead. The fast-moving lights were gone before they could be identified. The observers agreed, however, that they were neither meteors nor airplanes.

About an hour later the lights came back again but in a different formation and still later that night, they appeared for a third time. During each appearance they moved swiftly and silently from north to south. Judging their size, altitude and speed was almost impossible because there were no reference points in the nighttime sky. However, the professors hazarded the guess that the lights were of tremendous size. They placed their altitude at anywhere from 5,000 to 50,000 feet and their speed at 1,800 to 18,000 miles an hour.

Intrigued by what he and his friends had seen, the geology professor gave the story to the local newspaper. Unlike many UFO reports that immediately produce other accounts of the same or a similar UFO, the professor's story at first produced no reaction. Several days later, however, a Lubbock college student and amateur photographer named Carl Hart, Jr., brought five pictures of flying lights to the newspaper.

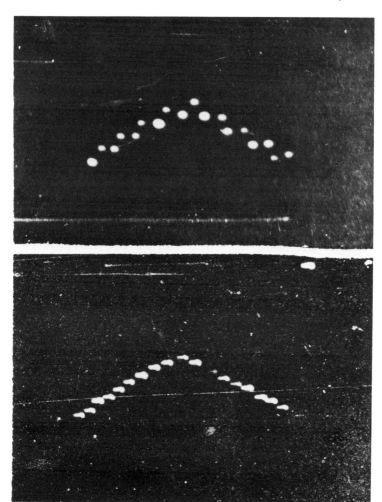

In 1951 the Lubbock lights puzzled many people in Texas. These photographs, taken by Carl Hart, Jr., show how the mysterious lights appeared in formation. Investigation revealed that the Lubbock lights were actually flights of plover.   UPI

He explained that he had seen the mysterious lights from his window the night before and recognized them as being similar to the lights seen by the professors. He had rushed out into the yard with his Kodak 35mm. camera, ready to take a picture if the lights reappeared. After a short wait the lights did reappear and Hart got two pictures. A few minutes later the lights were back and he shot three more photos.

Hart described the lights as brighter than Venus and flying in a perfect V-formation. He estimated that they traveled across the sky from north to south in four or five seconds.

After his staff photographer had examined Hart's negatives for evidence of a hoax, the newspaper editor published the pictures and they were given a wide circulation by United Press. Accompanying the pictures were stories about UFO sightings in Lubbock which had now increased in number and spread to the surrounding area.

During the ensuing weeks, hundreds of people claimed to have seen mysterious lights and many more saw Hart's photographs. There were suggestions that the lights were migrating birds or flying saucers or a clever hoax but in the absence of proof for any of these theories, the Lubbock lights remained a mystery.

Since the night when they first saw the lights, the college professors had seen them several more times. During their observations they made a serious attempt to determine the altitude, speed and size of the lights. Their efforts met with little success, however. The lights, moving over Lubbock with great speed, were difficult to track against the night sky. On several occasions the group traveled to the country hoping to find better viewing conditions. On these nights they saw no formations of lights although lights were reported over Lubbock. From the observations that they were able to make, however, the professors concluded that the lights were probably flying at an elevation of 2,000 to 3,000 feet instead of the 5,000 to 50,000 feet that they had estimated earlier.

In late September a report on the Lubbock lights reached the Air Force. Captain Edward J. Ruppelt, the Air Force officer who became the first director of Project Blue Book, traveled to Lubbock to investigate the case. Ruppelt later wrote a very good book about his experiences as a UFO investigator, called *The Report on Unidentified Flying Objects,* which includes the story of the Lubbock lights.

In Lubbock, Ruppelt interviewed the professors and learned that they thought the lights might be a natural phenomenon that had not been observed before. He visited Carl Hart who described the path of the lights across the sky and showed Ruppelt where he had taken the pictures. Captain Ruppelt also interviewed other observers of the mysterious lights in Lubbock and nearby towns. He found that, with a few exceptions, their descriptions were similar: There was a formation of glowing lights moving swiftly from north to south across the sky.

In Brownfield, a town 30 miles from Lubbock, Ruppelt interviewed an elderly rancher, a native Texan who was thoroughly familiar with the wildlife of the region. The rancher had read about the mysterious lights in the newspaper and watched for them. One night, three formations of lights flew over his house. It was while he was watching the third formation that he heard the unmistakable call of the plover, a water bird with a white breast and a one-foot wingspread. Moreover, this formation was low enough for him to actually see the birds.

Further investigation revealed that the oily white breast of a plover could easily reflect city lights. This would explain why the professors had seen nothing out in the dark countryside on nights when the flying lights were clearly visible in Lubbock. Captain Ruppelt also discovered that there were more plover than usual in the Lubbock area that fall.

With one exception, everything pointed to flights of plover as the explanation of the mysterious Lubbock lights. That exception was the five photographs taken by Carl Hart which did not appear to be of birds. Furthermore, the photographs did not match the professors' descriptions of what they had seen during their observations of the lights. The photographs raised other questions as well. Although it was a clear night, no stars were visible in any of the backgrounds. And Hart had managed to take his photographs in a remarkably short time. What was even more puzzling, the pattern of the lights indicated that all of the photographs must have been taken as the V-formation of lights approached the camera.

Air Force investigators finally set the photographs aside because not enough data was available to determine if they were authentic or a fraud. As for the visual sightings of the Lubbock lights, the observers had, beyond any doubt, seen not UFOs but plover.

During the spring of 1966 many residents of Michigan were convinced that low-flying UFOs had invaded the south-eastern part of their state. The first report came from the village of Dexter. On the evening of March 20, Frank Mannor and his family were watching television when the family dogs began to bark. Mannor went out to quiet them. As he turned back toward the house, he saw what he at first thought was a meteor about half a mile away. However, after he watched what looked like a ball of fire stop, settle to the ground and then rise slightly, he changed his mind. The ball of fire finally came to rest behind some trees in a nearby swamp where a ruddy glow marked its location. Mannor called his family and they, too, could plainly see the red glow.

Accompanied by his son, Ronnie, Mannor set off into the swamp toward the strange red glow. They were wearing boots but their progress was slow as they moved through the mud and muck of the dark swamp. Finally, they came to a small hill. From its top they saw a pyramid-shaped object about 500 yards away. They reported later that the object was "like a yellowish coral rock and looked like it had holes in it." The father and son could not make out many details, however, because of the distance and the shimmering heat waves that surrounded the pyramid. They did observe a blue-green light on one side and a white light on the other. As they started to move closer the white light changed to a bloody red, a sight that made Ronnie call out, "Look at that horrible thing!" At this point the object disappeared.

Meanwhile, the Dexter police and the Washtenaw County sheriff had been informed of the mysterious red glow in the swamp and both organizations dispatched men to the Man-

93

nor home. When the policemen and sheriff's deputies searched the swamp, several of them saw weird, flickering lights that vanished when an observer approached.

The next night there was another report of mysterious glowing lights. It came from Hillsdale College, 63 miles from Dexter, where 85 girls saw moving lights that alternated from red to white in Slayton Arboretum, near their dormitory. The students turned off the study lamps in their rooms to improve visibility as they watched the lights which remained close to the ground, pulsating and moving from side to side.

During their vigil the girls kept a record of what they observed. Some of the students thought they saw a disclike shape between two lights; others saw a series of lights between two end lights, one of which alternated between red and white while the other remained a flickering blue-green.

Soon after they first observed the lights, the girls notified their housemother and the county civil defense director, both of whom joined the students in watching the lights from dormitory windows overlooking the arboretum. However, Hillsdale patrolmen, who drove down a road near the arboretum, were unable to see any lights at all. Whenever a patrol car approached, the lights disappeared; when the car passed, the lights returned. No one attempted to search the arboretum on foot. It was 2:30 A.M. when the lights faded. They did not reappear that night.

Project Blue Book sent its representative to Michigan on March 22. He was Dr. J. Allen Hynek, an astronomer who had been a scientific consultant to the project since 1948. On March 23, Dr. Hynek interviewed Frank Mannor and his son, and the policeman and sheriff's deputies who had seen the lights in the swamp at Dexter. The next day, Dr. Hynek went to Hillsdale College to talk with the students who had seen the maneuvering lights in the arboretum. At the college he learned that on the previous night, pranksters had tried to generate a new UFO report by setting off flares and fireworks in the arboretum. The girls had not been fooled by the prank, however, and they were eager to tell Dr. Hynek about the real UFOs. They showed him the notes they had made of their observations, drew sketches and tried to estimate sizes and distances for the investigator. Dr. Hynek also talked with the civil defense director and he made a short visit to the arboretum.

Within a few days, Dr. Hynek had reached a tentative conclusion about the lights seen at Dexter and Hillsdale. In both cases the sightings had been made in a swampy area. Most of the observers had reported silent, glowing lights near the ground, lights that moved but never traveled very far. Frank Mannor and his son, the only two observers who claimed to have seen an actual object, had been 500 yards away from it in a dark swamp. They had, however, clearly seen red, white and blue-green lights, the same colors reported at Hillsdale.

When his investigation was completed, Dr. Hynek held a press conference in Detroit. In his statement to newsmen he suggested that burning swamp gas was the most likely explanation of the UFO reports from Dexter and Hillsdale. Hynek explained how decaying organic matter in swamps and marshes releases gases which can be ignited by spontaneous combustion or lightning. Moreover, gases trapped by winter ice are released in the spring and more burning is apt to occur then. Both the Dexter and the Hillsdale sightings took place in March.

Burning swamp gas (also called ignis fatuus, jack-o'-lanterns or will-o'-the-wisp) produces no heat. As a result, neither the ground nor the underbrush is set afire. The flames seem to be flickering over the ground or floating above it but they are actually going out in one place and reappearing in another, giving the illusion of motion. There is no smell and no sound except for an occasional pop when a flame appears.

Since he had arrived too late to observe the mysterious lights himself, it was impossible for Dr. Hynek to obtain definite evidence in the Dexter and Hillsdale cases. However, everything pointed to burning swamp gas as the explanation, and both the season of the year and the weather on the nights of the sightings supported that explanation. At the same time, investigation had revealed nothing to support the UFO theory that was popular with many residents of the area.

"It appears very likely," concluded Dr. Hynek, "that the combination of the conditions of this particular winter and the particular weather conditions that night—it was clear and there was little wind at either location—were such as to have produced this unusual and puzzling display."

The Dexter and Hillsdale UFOs were, in all probability, burning swamp gas.

Several of our astronauts have seen UFOs from their spaceships as they traveled far above the surface of the earth.

While no information is available on sightings by the Soviet Union's cosmonauts, they have probably seen UFOs, too. In the case of the astronauts, almost all of the sightings have eventually been identified.

American astronauts are selected from highly qualified groups of test pilots and scientists and they are trained observers. A spacecraft, however, is not the most ideal vehicle from which to make observations. It has been compared to a closed car with no side or rear windows and a partially covered, smudged windshield. Spacecraft windows are small and they provide only a limited forward view. If the astronauts wish to see to their right, left or rear, they must turn the spacecraft, a maneuver that consumes valuable fuel. Moreover, spacecraft windows tend to collect deposits from gases released during the firing of third-stage rockets and other sources. The smudging that results reduces visibility, especially in bright daylight. Nevertheless, the astronauts have observed a wide variety of strange sights during their space flights. Some they immediately identified as man-made objects or natural phenomena but others were reported as UFOs.

One of the earliest UFO reports from space came from John Glenn, the astronaut who made Project Mercury's first manned orbital space flight. The astronaut called the sighting "the biggest surprise of the flight."

Glenn's Mercury spacecraft was moving into dawn on its first orbit of the earth and sunlight had just touched the capsule when the astronaut glanced out of the window into a swarm of luminous particles. This is how he described them:

Project Mercury Astronaut Scott Carpenter photographed these bright objects from his Aurora 7 spacecraft. They were identified as ice crystals that had formed on the spacecraft and broken off. The light at upper right is the sun. **NASA**

"These particles were a light yellowish-green color. It was as if the spacecraft were moving through a field of fireflies. They were about the brightness of a first magnitude star and appeared to vary in size from a pinhead up to possibly ⅜ inch. They were about 8 to 10 feet apart and evenly distributed through the space around the spacecraft and across the window, drifting very, very slowly, and would then gradually move off, back in the direction I was looking."

Glenn observed the particles for approximately four minutes and he saw them again each time his spacecraft moved from darkness into sunlight as it traveled around the earth. Scott Carpenter, another Mercury astronaut, saw similar particles during his space flight and they were also reported by several of the Gemini astronauts.

UFOs observed by astronauts during space flights were investigated by the National Aeronautics and Space Administration (NASA) rather than Project Blue Book. After studying the report received from John Glenn, NASA scientists identified the mysterious particles as millimeter-size flakes liberated at or near sunrise by the spacecraft itself. Observations made on subsequent flights confirmed this explanation.

Powerful rockets boost NASA's manned capsules into space from their launching pad at Cape Kennedy. When these rockets have exhausted their fuel they are discarded. Mercury and Gemini third-stage rockets were discarded at such a high altitude that they went into an earth orbit of their own and the astronauts often saw them as they traveled through space. Of course the astronauts knew they were seeing spent boosters and not UFOs.

During the two-man Project Gemini space flights, the astronauts discarded equipment that was no longer needed. They did this by tossing the items out of an open hatch while the capsule was depressurized. Such things as tethers, hoses and food scraps were disposed of in this way. Like the spent boosters, discards from the capsule went into an earth orbit and they were sometimes observed later from the spacecraft. But in this case, too, the astronauts quickly identified the orbiting objects as their own discards. Astronauts have also seen and identified debris from previous space shots.

Since the Soviet Union launched Sputnik I, the first man-made earth satellite, in 1957, hundreds of artificial satellites have gone into orbit. When their own orbit brings them close enough, astronauts see these satellites. Because the path of a satellite is known, such sightings are quickly identified, either by the astronauts themselves or by scientists on the ground. On three occasions, however, a sure identification could not be made from the information that was available.

During the flight of Gemini 4, Astronaut James McDivitt saw a cylindrical object with "big arms sticking out." The arms resembled an antenna. The object itself was white or silvery but McDivitt could not tell how far away it was. The astronaut took both still and motion pictures which, when developed, showed only a hazy image.

Investigation revealed that Pegasus 2, a satellite with winglike extensions launched by NASA to study micro-meteoroids, was 1,250 miles from Gemini 4 at the time of the sighting. While Pegasus 2 somewhat resembled McDivitt's description of "big arms sticking out," the satellite would have been too far away for him to see it clearly. Moreover, the Gemini 4 astronauts were unable to see Pegasus 2 when its path brought it much closer to their spacecraft.

Astronaut McDivitt thought he had seen an unmanned satellite but the ten objects in addition to Pegasus 2, known to be in space at the time, were all too small and far away to match McDivitt's description.

Astronaut McDivitt saw a second UFO during his Gemini 4 space flight. He described it as a moving bright light "very high . . . just like a star on the ground when you see one go by, a long way away." The light was higher than the spacecraft and moving from south to north. McDivitt thought it might be another satellite, but it could not be positively identified as any of those known to be in earth orbit.

During the Gemini 7 space flight, Astronaut Frank Borman saw the third UFO. At the beginning of Gemini 7's second orbit he called NASA ground controllers at the Manned Spacecraft Center in Houston, Texas, and reported, "Bogey at 10 o'clock high." Bogey is a term used by airmen which means unidentified aircraft. The astronaut also had the Gemini 7 booster in sight and what Borman described as "very, very many—looks like hundreds of little particles banked on the left out about 3 to 7 miles." Neither the bogey nor the particles could be identified.

The unidentified sightings during the Gemini 4 and Gemini 7 space flights are but a very small fraction of the total number of sightings that have been reported by our astronauts. As in the case of UFOs seen closer to the earth, most UFOs reported from space have been identified when enough information about them was available.

8

Billions of Worlds

In 1938 there was no television for people to watch. Instead, they gathered around their radio sets and listened to their favorite programs. On the night of October 30, 1938, when actor-producer Orson Welles presented a radio drama based on *The War of the Worlds* by British author H. G. Wells, a large audience tuned in. *The War of the Worlds* was about an invasion of the earth by Martians and Mr. Welles used news bulletins, interviews and realistic sound effects to tell the story. In fact, the dramatization was so real that thousands of listeners were convinced that Martians armed with a deadly "heat-ray" had landed in New Jersey.

Panic spread across the country as people rushed out of their houses to escape the approaching Martians. Some ran aimlessly through city streets; others got into their cars and headed for the country. The police and the military forces received so many phone calls that communications broke down in some areas. The radio network received calls, too, and an announcer went on the air to assure listeners that there was no cause for alarm. After some hours, calm was restored.

Orson Welles's dramatic presentation of an imaginary Martian invasion and the panic that resulted renewed interest in two questions that had long perplexed scientists: Are there other inhabited worlds besides our own? Could those inhabitants travel to the earth?

Our earth is one of nine planets that revolves around a star that we call the sun. The sun, in turn, is one of hundreds of billions of stars that makes up the galazy called the Milky Way. And beyond our own galaxy there are billions of other star clusters in the vastness of space. The earth, then, is but a very, very small part of an unimaginably large universe.

Before the invention of the telescope, man knew nothing more about the universe than what he could see with his own eyes. He saw the sun, the moon, the five visible planets and many stars, all of which seemed to move around the earth. Understandably enough, to ancient man the earth was the center of the universe.

Copernicus, a Polish astronomer who lived from 1473 until 1543, was the first to successfully challenge this idea. His studies convinced him that revolution around the sun offered a better explanation for the observed movements of the heavenly bodies than revolution around the earth. He also suggested that the earth daily rotated on its axis from west to east. Not everyone agreed with Copernicus, of course. To many scholars the idea that the sun, not the earth, was the center of the universe seemed heretical. And so did the idea that the earth was moving in space.

Until 1609, astronomers studied the movements of the heavenly bodies without the help of the telescope. This valuable instrument was invented in Holland by a spectacle maker who discovered that when he looked through two spectacle lenses held a short distance apart, objects appeared nearer and larger. The Italian astronomer Galileo Galilei heard about the telescope in 1609 and made several for himself, each one more powerful than the last. By 1610 he had developed a telescope powerful enough to reveal the satellites of the planet Jupiter, the spots on the sun, the craterous surface of the moon and the phases of Venus. Much of what Galileo saw through his telescope supported the theories of Copernicus and both men are listed among the founders of modern astronomy.

Galileo also studied the Milky Way through his telescope and observed that it was a collection of distant stars. It was to be some time before much more was learned about it, and even today information about our galaxy is in short supply because of the great distances involved and because parts of it are hidden by clouds of dust and gas. We know that the Milky Way is a flat belt of billions of stars and solar systems some 80,000 light-years in diameter. (A light-year is the distance over which light can travel in a year at 186,000 miles a second, or approximately six trillion miles.) Our own sun is located some 26,000 light-years from the center of the Milky Way. The nearest star in the Milky Way, Proxima Centauri, is 4.3 light-years from the earth. There are only fifteen stars within 11.5 light-years of the star that we call the sun.

Many of the stars in the Milky Way could conceivably be

accompanied by planets, just as our sun is, and some of these planets might be able to support life. When we ask if any of that life could visit the earth, however, a number of seemingly insurmountable obstacles present themselves. Even in the case of the fifteen stars closest to the sun, the distance to the earth from a planet outside our own solar system is almost too great to be imagined. And it is entirely possible that in no one of the closest fifteen solar systems is civilization at a stage where interstellar travel would be likely.

Scientists do agree that life is possible—in fact, they say it is probable—in solar systems besides our own. If physical and chemical conditions are right, life should emerge just as it did on earth more than a billion years ago. Man himself has been on earth for perhaps 100,000 years but life might have developed differently on planets in other solar systems. Because we have no way of observing planets outside of our own solar system, we have no way of knowing what form life has taken elsewhere or how far it has progressed.

On a planet in another solar system there might be intelligent life with the capability for interstellar travel but no interest in it. Or there might be life that has not yet developed the technology to make such travel possible. We just don't know enough about the possible inhabitants of other solar systems and other galaxies to make estimates of what they can and cannot do. But it does not seem reasonable, in view of the great distances and other problems involved, to expect them to pay us a surprise visit any time soon.

Has one of the other planets in our solar system developed a civilization capable of sending spaceships to the earth?

When we consider this question we have more information to work with. The planets of our solar system are much, much closer to earth than the planets of other solar systems and we have learned more about them.

Pluto, the outermost of the known planets in our solar system, has an irregular orbit, but its average distance from the sun—3,671,000,000 miles—is infinitesimal compared with the nearest star in the Milky Way. Since Pluto was discovered in 1930 we have learned that its diameter is only 3,700 miles, making it one of the smallest of the planets. The earth's diameter is 7,918 miles. It takes 248 earth-years for Pluto to make one revolution around the sun. Because of its faintness, small size and distance from the earth, Pluto can only be seen with the help of powerful telescopes and there is still much to be learned about its chemical makeup, composition and atmosphere. However, because of its great distance from the sun, it would appear that Pluto is too cold to support life.

The next four planets in order of distance from the sun— Neptune, Uranus, Saturn and Jupiter—are also too cold to support any known form of life. Moreover, they are huge balls of swirling hydrogen, methane, ammonia and other gases whose solid surfaces exist only at great depths. Astronomers sometimes refer to them as "gas giants."

Jupiter, the largest of the gas giants, is 88,770 miles in diameter. Its average distance from the sun is 483,000,000 miles and it takes Jupiter 11.86 years to travel around the sun once. While Jupiter is revolving around the sun, no less than twelve moons are revolving around the planet. They do not all travel at the same speed, however.

Saturn, the next largest of the gas giants, has nine moons of its own and is surrounded by a system of rings as well. The rings, which were first seen but not identified by Galileo, are thought to be composed of particles of unknown size. Saturn's average distance from the sun is 885,900,000 miles and it travels around that body once every 29.5 years. Saturn's diameter measures 71,500 miles.

Uranus and Neptune are considerably smaller than the other two gas giants. Uranus has a diameter of 29,500 miles and Neptune a diameter of 27,600 miles. The orbit of Uranus carries it far from the sun; its average distance is 1,783,700,000 miles. It travels around the sun once every 84 years. Neptune's orbit carries it even farther from the sun than that of Uranus. Neptune's average distance is 2,796,700,000 miles, approximately thirty times farther than the earth. It's temperature may be as low as 337° Fahrenheit below zero.

While we can safely say that no life as we know it could exist in the deep chill of Pluto, Jupiter, Saturn, Uranus and Neptune, the planets Mercury, Venus and Mars are closer to the sun and therefore warmer. Moreover, they are composed of the same kind of material that makes up the earth. Along with the earth they are called terrestrial planets.

Conditions favorable to life are not to be found on all terrestrial planets, however. Mercury, the planet closest to the sun, is too hot to support life. Its average distance from the sun is only 36 million miles, compared with almost 93 million miles for the earth. Moreover, Mercury travels around the sun in 88 days, but it takes 59 days to rotate once on its axis, a very slow rotation that exposes the same side of the planet to the sun for long periods. On Mercury's sun side, temperatures can climb as high as 770° Fahrenheit, hot enough to melt lead. The other side of the planet is very cold, perhaps as cold as 450° below zero. At that temperature hydrogen and oxygen become liquids and carbon dioxide freezes. Mercury is only a little larger than the moon. Its small size and high temperatures indicate that it has no atmosphere, at least on its bright side. If life exists on Mercury, it must be very different from life on earth.

Although Venus is farther from the sun than Mercury—its average distance is 67,270,000 miles—the planet is also probably too hot for advanced forms of life. Moreover, Venus appears to have little, if any, oxygen and water vapor in its atmosphere. Venus is only slightly smaller than the earth and it is the closest to the earth of any of the planets. Its average distance from us is only 24,600,000 miles. In spite of its closeness, however, we know relatively little about Venus because it is hidden from the earth by a thick veil of clouds. Astronomers can't study the surface of the planet with a telescope, but both the United States and the Soviet Union have sent unmanned space probes to the vicinity of Venus and radar beams have been bounced off the Venusian surface. These investigations have indicated that Venus is an unlikely place for intelligent life to have developed, but the possibility of life there has not been ruled out.

Mars has long been considered the planet most likely to harbor some form of life and "Martian," meaning an inhabitant of Mars, has become a part of our language. While we have yet to see a Martian, we have learned quite a bit about the planet.

Mars is smaller than the earth. Its diameter is only 4,200 miles compared with 7,918 miles for the earth. The planet's small size accounts for its thin atmosphere. There isn't enough gravity on Mars to keep the gases that make up the atmosphere from being lost in space. The Martian atmosphere does contain traces of oxygen and water vapor, however, and both are needed to support life. About three-quarters of Mars appears to be orange-colored. Such areas are generally thought to be deserts. The remaining one-quarter of the Martian surface is also dry, but it is a gray or brown color that changes with the seasons. The colors become darker in the summer and fade during the winter and may indicate some form of plant life.

During its year of 687 days, Mars travels in an orbit that varies from 128 million to 155 million miles from the sun. It is farther from the sun than the earth and colder. During the Martian day, which is about as long as our day, temperatures may rise to 90° Fahrenheit at the equator. At night, however, the Martian temperature may drop as low as a freezing 95° below zero. This results from the planet's distance from the sun and also from its thin atmosphere and the absence of large bodies of water which would help retain heat.

Mars is a bright planet that can be seen without a telescope. With the help of a telescope, astronomers have been able to observe many details of the Martian surface. The astronomer Christian Huygens, who lived during the seventeenth century, was the first to note the ice caps on the Martian poles which grow larger during the Martian fall and winter and shrink in the spring and summer.

In 1877, the Italian astronomer Giovanni Schiaparelli observed the feature that has caused the most speculation about possible life on Mars. Through his powerful telescope, Schiaparelli saw a network of straight lines stretching across the Martian surface in geometric patterns. The astronomer estimated that some of the lines might be as long as 1,500 miles and 25 miles wide. He applied the Italian word *canali* to his discovery and the word became canals in English.

Schiaparelli was cautious about inferring that the *canali* were the work of intelligent beings, but to some astronomers they were proof that life did exist on Mars. The American astronomer Percival Lowell, for one, concluded that Schiaparelli's lines were bands of land irrigated by canals, the product of a technically advanced society. Other astronomers disagreed, however, and in 1965 photos transmitted by NASA's Mariner 4 as it streaked past Mars showed no canals. The Mariner photos did show a dry, craterous surface that resembled the surface of the moon.

Mars has two small moons of its own named Phobos and Deimos which travel around Mars in circular orbits instead of following the usual elliptical path of revolving bodies. This and other peculiarities in the behavior of Phobos and Deimos have led some astronomers to speculate that they might be artificial satellites placed in orbit by obviously intelligent Martians.

Both the Soviet Union and the United States have sent unmanned space probes to the vicinity of Mars. Of these,

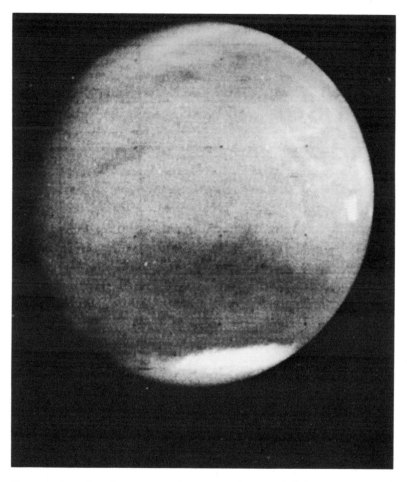

Photographs taken by unmanned space probes are helping us learn more about the planets in our solar system. Mariner 6 took this photograph of Mars in July 1969, when it was 282,000 miles from that planet. NASA

the United States' Mariner 6 and Mariner 7 have provided the most information. Reaching the vicinity of Mars just five days apart in 1969, the two space probes sent back valuable photographs from as close as 2,000 miles above the Martian surface. While information obtained from Mariner 6, Mariner 7 and the earlier Mariner 4 has confirmed astronomers' suspicions that conditions on Mars are harsh, they do not appear to be harsh enough to preclude the development of life. Moreover, at some time in the past Mars may have been warmer and surrounded by a heavier atmosphere making the development of life even more likely. Future space probes will tell us more about Mars and someday NASA plans to send astronauts there for an on-the-spot inspection. At the present time it appears to be the planet most likely to support life in some form, perhaps some kind of plant life. However, there is no evidence that life there has developed to a stage that would support the technology required for space travel.

Some scientists think that civilizations on other worlds, if they exist, will attempt to contact us by radio instead of traveling to the earth in a spaceship. In 1960 a group of these scientists organized Project Ozma (named for the Princess of the Land of Oz) to listen for radio signals from space. They listened with a huge radio telescope at the National Radio Astronomy Observatory at Green Bank, West Virginia. A radio telescope "sees" radio waves instead of light rays and it can penetrate great distances. Moreover, clouds and dust don't affect it as they do an ordinary telescope.

Mariner 7's photograph of the south polar cap of Mars was taken from 3,300 miles above the Martian surface. It shows some fairly large craters and what is believed to be the south pole (lower left). NASA

Project Ozma astronomers decided to limit their research to the stars Tau Ceti, 11.2 light-years from the earth, and Epsilon Eridani, 10.7 light-years away. They appear to be stars very much like our sun and they probably have planets revolving around them although the planets cannot be seen.

If the inhabitants of these planets did send out a radio signal it would take 11 years to reach the earth and another 11 years for an answer to be returned.

The astronomers at Green Bank reasoned that signals dispatched by intelligent life on Tau Ceti or Epsilon Eridani would contain a pattern of some sort to distinguish them from random radio noise. This is what they were listening for when they pointed the huge Green Bank antenna at Epsilon Eridani on April 8, 1960. And that is what they heard: a series of spaced pulses quite unlike the random signals they normally received. The excitement that gripped Project Ozma was short-lived, however. Within two weeks the spaced signal was traced to a secret military experiment involving radar—not on Epsilon Eridani, but on earth. Project Ozma continued for several more weeks until the Green Bank radio telescope was needed for other research. No signals from space were received.

In 1967, steady radio pulses were picked up by a radio telescope in England and they were also noted by astronomers elsewhere. For a time it was thought that the mysterious pulses might be a message from another planet but they were finally identified as coming from neutron stars. Such stars—astronomers call them pulsars—are old stars that have exploded and they are capable of giving off large amounts of energy.

Someday a signal may reach the earth from one of the billions of worlds that surround our own. Or astronomers may discover some other evidence of intelligent life on another planet. Until then, they can only tell us that the probability of life existing elsewhere is very great. But they also tell us that there is little possibility of contact between the earth and planets outside our own solar system. And even within our solar system the prospects of contact are slight.

9

How Do Scientists Explain UFOs?

If astronomers, the scientists who specialize in the study of the universe, think it is highly unlikely that unidentified flying objects are interstellar or interplanetary spaceships, how do scientists explain the true UFOs? These are the UFOs about which reliable witnesses have reported enough information to make investigation possible, yet the UFOs cannot be readily identified as man-made objects, natural phenomena or hoaxes. Most of these mysterious sightings, some scientists suggest, may be atmospheric effects about which very little is known.

Plasmas, luminous concentrations of electrified gas molecules, are an atmospheric phenomenon that science has just begun to investigate. The lightning that streaks across the sky from one electrically charged cloud to another during thunderstorms is a form of plasma. So is the much rarer ball lightning, a bright ball of electrified gas that the Germans call *Kugelblitz.* The balls may be anywhere from a few inches to several feet in diameter. They range from reddish-orange to bluish-white in color and look and act like solid objects. They have been observed hanging motionless in the air and moving near the ground and at high altitudes. The luminous spheres remain visible anywhere from a few seconds to several minutes.

The exact origin of plasmas is unknown, although ordinary lightning is associated with electrical discharges during thunderstorms. Clear-air turbulence and pollutants in the atmosphere may trigger other plasmas. Some plasmas appear to originate along high-tension electric lines, especially when the lines and their insulators are covered with dust or salt deposits. Electrical engineers call such a discharge power line corona.

Electrical engineer Philip Klass, who is an editor of the magazine *Aviation Week & Space Technology,* thinks that many UFOs may be plasmas and he has written a book entitled *UFOs—Identified* in which he explains his theory.

Klass developed his plasma theory after reading John Fuller's book, *Incident at Exeter.* Before Klass read the book, he was convinced that UFOs were either common objects such as airplanes or stars seen under unusual conditions or outright hoaxes. He began to change his mind when he realized that the descriptions of the Exeter UFOs described plasmas as well. The colors, shapes and movements of the UFOs and the duration of the sightings all pointed to plasmas as the logical explanation. He also noted that many of the sightings had taken place near power lines. Moreover, Exeter had experienced a very dry summer and the area was close enough to the Atlantic Ocean for salt to have coated the lines. Before he finished *Incident at Exeter,* the editor had decided to investigate the possibility that Norman Muscarello and the others had seen some form of plasma.

During his research, Klass carefully analyzed the UFO reports from Exeter as they were recorded in Fuller's book. His analysis confirmed his original impression that many of the UFOs were, in fact, plasmas. Klass also studied NICAP's *The UFO Evidence* and concluded that his plasma theory would explain the otherwise puzzling variety of UFO shapes, sizes and colors reported in that publication. It also explained the sudden appearance and disappearance of many UFOs and their erratic flight characteristics.

According to Klass, plasma can be picked up on a radar screen where it is apt to appear as a strong blip that disappears suddenly. But instead of zooming off at a very high speed the plasma has simply dissipated its electrical charge and merged with the surrounding air. Klass suggests that plasmas may have been responsible for the famous radar sightings in Washington during the July 1952 UFO flap, and for other mysterious radar sightings as well.

Another much-publicized UFO that can be explained as a form of plasma is the one reported by Lonnie Zamora in 1964. To check out his theory, Klass traveled to Socorro, New Mexico, where he interviewed Zamora and others involved in the case. He also examined the gully where the UFO had landed. Significantly, there was a 115,000-volt high-tension line a mile west of the gully.

When Klass left Socorro he was convinced that Lonnie

Zamora had seen a plasma. The police officer's description of a "bluish and sort of orange" flame and of a "whitish" object would fit a plasma. As for the two figures in white coveralls, they might have been wisps of electrified gas that Zamora mistook for small men from a distance. By substituting plasma for the spaceship explanation, Klass was able to clear up most of the mysteries of the Socorro sighting. According to Klass, plasmas have been responsible for high-level as well as low-level UFO sightings. He explains that as a plane moves through the air, it may accumulate an electrical charge which, when discharged, appears as a ball of fire. The World War II "foo-fighters" were probably plasmas as are the many glowing UFOs reported by postwar pilots.

While Philip Klass does not claim that all UFOs are plasmas, he does feel that his theory explains many of them.

Dr. Donald H. Menzel, an astronomer and astrophysicist, is another scientist who has devoted considerable time to the study of UFOs. He thinks that most UFO reports result from the observer's misinterpretation of what he has seen. A book which Menzel wrote with Lyle G. Boyd, called *The World of Flying Saucers*, contains numerous examples of such mistaken identification. In a case involving what the authors call the "flying bird cage," a Michigan couple saw a strange object hovering about two miles from the road on which they were traveling. The UFO was oval in shape with a domed top that made it look like a bird cage. Two shafts of pale-yellow light illuminated the object from bottom to top. It appeared to be from 20 to 30 feet in diameter and about 200 feet from the ground as it traveled parallel with the road. After keeping pace for a mile or so, the UFO's yellow lights grew dim and a circle of red light appeared on its bottom. The UFO then rose very rapidly and vanished.

This UFO turned out to be a floodlit radio telescope belonging to the University of Michigan. A wire-mesh structure beneath the telescope's 85-foot "dish" made the UFO look like a bird cage. As the couple drove along the highway, the telescope only appeared to be moving along with the car. But it was sweeping the sky from the horizon to a point directly overhead and as it swung upward, its yellow lights were gradually obscured. The red lights, on the other hand, belonged to a radio tower located between the telescope and the witnesses. When the floodlights illuminating the telescope were turned off by the astronomers who had finished their night's work, it completed the illusion that a UFO had changed its lights from yellow to red and vanished.

UFO investigators were able to quickly identify the flying bird cage. Sometimes, however, identifying a UFO is difficult, or even impossible, because little reliable information is available. Nevertheless, writes Dr. Menzel, if enough facts are known, UFOs can almost always be identified as common, everyday objects seen under unusual circumstances or the result of natural phenomena unfamiliar to the person who reported the UFO.

Both Philip J. Klass and Dr. Menzel say they are keeping an open mind about the possibility of visitors from another planet at some time in the future. It could happen, they admit. But, they add, it hasn't happened yet.

Dr. J. Allen Hynek, the astronomical consultant to Project Blue Book, agrees with Klass and Menzel that at this time there is no scientific evidence to support the theory that some UFOs are interstellar or interplanetary spaceships. In 1966, when he was asked by a member of the House Armed Services Committee if UFOs could be extraterrestrial visitors, Hynek replied: "I have not seen any evidence to confirm this, nor have I known any competent scientist who has, or believes that any kind of extraterrestrial intelligence is involved. However, the possibility should be kept open as a possible hypothesis. I don't believe we should ever close our minds to it."

Dr. James E. McDonald, a University of Arizona atmospheric physicist, is a scientist who takes the opposite point of view. In 1968 he told the House Committee on Space and Astronautics: "My own present opinion, based on two years of careful study, is that UFOs are probably extraterrestrial devices engaged in something that might be tentatively termed 'surveillance.' "

McDonald has examined hundreds of UFO reports made by reliable observers and he argues that there are many well-documented sightings that can't be explained as natural phenomena, hoaxes or mistakes on the part of observers. "I think that UFOs are the number one problem of world science," he says.

Carl J. Jung, the noted psychiatrist, has given us a different explanation of UFO reports. In a book called *Flying Saucers: A Modern Myth of Things Seen in the Skies,* written in 1959, he suggests that UFO sightings are the psychological result of the many problems that have plagued the human race since World War II, especially the nuclear bomb which has given man the capability of destroying the earth. To certain worried people, flying saucers may represent a source of salvation. Once man would have turned to religion for comfort, Dr. Jung writes, but in an age when technological advance has made space flight possible, he turns to the UFO.

Scientists became directly involved in a full-scale investigation of UFOs in 1966 when the University of Colorado agreed to carry out an independent study of selected sightings. Working under a half-million-dollar contract with the United States Air Force, the university assembled a staff of twelve astronomers, physicists and psychologists for the project and chose Dr. Edward U. Condon as its scientific director. Dr. Condon was a professor of physics at the University of Colorado and a former director of the National Bureau of Standards. Although it was supplying funds for the study, the Air Force guaranteed that the Colorado Project would have complete freedom in carrying out its investigations. Moreover, at the conclusion of the study, the results were to be reviewed by the prestigious National Academy of Sciences as a further independent check on the scientific validity of the investigation.

Over a two-year period the Colorado Project studied hundreds of UFO reports, most of them new, although some older sightings were included. Project Blue Book made its files available to the Colorado investigators. NICAP and APRO also supplied material and suggestions as did Dr. James E. McDonald who was conducting his own investigation of UFOs. In addition, the Colorado Project looked into

UFO investigating activities abroad, especially in those countries that had official programs.

For the purposes of its study the Colorado Project defined a UFO as the stimulus for a report made by one or more individuals of something seen in the sky, or an object thought to be capable of flight but landed on the earth, that the observer could not identify as having an ordinary natural origin. The report could be made to police, government officials, the press, one of the private UFO investigating organizations or directly to the Colorado Project. When a report was selected for investigation, a two-man team was usually assigned to the case. If possible, one of the investigators was trained in physical science and the other in psychology.

In the case of new reports, the Project attempted to send a team of investigators to the location of the sighting within twenty-four hours after a report was received. Unless there were discrepancies in the records, few field trips were made to check on old sightings. The investigators quickly discovered that they could obtain little new, reliable information from witnesses who had seen a UFO five, ten or more years earlier. Instead, the Project tried to develop other sources of information such as weather data. In both old and new cases the objective of the Colorado investigation was to obtain useful information about UFO phenomena and cases were selected for study with that objective in mind.

One of the old cases investigated by the Colorado Project involved pieces of metal supposedly dropped from a spaceship in 1957. The metal, in the form of short, narrow strips, was sent to the Project's headquarters in Boulder, Colorado, by a man who claimed that it had been highly radioactive when he found it on the day after he had seen two spaceships hovering overhead. Along with the metal, he sent a laboratory report stating that the material was primarily aluminum.

Since the metal sample was the important evidence in the case, the Colorado Project sent it to a research and engineering company for analysis. The sample was promptly identified as radar chaff manufactured by a company in Brooklyn, New York. Radar chaff, which consists of strips of aluminum foil coated with lead powder, was developed during World War II when it was dropped from aircraft to confuse enemy radar. Since then, it has been used for experiments involving radar. The chaff in question could have been dropped from an airplane testing ground radar. But it could also have been dropped from a balloon, which would explain the spaceship part of the UFO report. In any case, the pieces of metal came from Brooklyn, not another planet.

When Colorado Project representatives investigated new UFO reports, they usually found that the UFO was no longer there when they arrived on the scene. Since the UFO had vanished, information about it could be acquired only by interviewing witnesses and examining the area where the sighting took place. In one case, however, UFOs remained on view long enough for the investigators to see them in action.

The nighttime sightings of strange, orange-white lights near Coarsegold, California, had been recurring for several months when the Colorado Project heard about them. During that period, residents of the area had photographed the

UFOs and recorded descriptions and data on the times and durations of their sightings. To add to the mystery, NICAP representatives had investigated the UFOs and failed to identify them.

On their second night in Coarsegold, the Project field team saw bright orange-white lights similar to the ones that had been reported previously. Lights that hovered, moved horizontally and then vanished were seen on the next night as well. The investigators thought that the lights might be aircraft but the nearest Air Force base denied any knowledge of air traffic in the vicinity of Coarsegold on either night.

On the third night one of the Colorado investigators went to the highest fire-lookout tower in the area. From there he saw a succession of lights that appeared to brighten, dim, vanish and reappear as they moved back and forth over the valley below. Lights came together and separated, hovered and moved off. It was what area residents called a good, solid UFO sighting.

From his observation point in the tower, the Project investigator became convinced that the lights were aircraft. Using binoculars he could make out something that looked like a runway where planes were taxiing, taking off, circling and landing. The next night he moved closer to the air base and saw the same orange-white lights, but now he could see that they belonged to aircraft.

Another check with officials at the air base revealed that the base did have planes in the air when the UFOs were observed. Its aerial tankers and B-52s regularly practiced refueling at night. Moreover, the planes carried powerful spotlights which were switched on and off during the refueling operation. It was these lights that the residents of Coarsegold and the Colorado Project's investigators had seen.

The Colorado Project considered the Coarsegold sightings a good example of how ordinary airborne objects, such as tankers and B-52s, can, by unusual behavior and lighting, convince observers that they are seeing UFOs. Unfortunately, in this case identification was made more difficult by incorrect information from the air base.

Not all of the UFOs investigated by the Colorado Project could be identified. One puzzling case, reported to the Project in the spring of 1967, involved a UFO that seemed to interfere with the operation of an automobile. Such interference, which can take the form of a stalled engine or headlights and radios that won't work, has been a baffling part of many UFO reports.

In the case investigated by the Colorado Project, a secretary was driving at night in a 1964 Comet when she noticed that the road in front of her seemed unusually bright. Thinking that her own headlights were responsible, she operated the foot switch to dim them and then turned the headlights completely off. The road remained illuminated. At this point she became aware of a glowing object hovering over her car. She reported that she could see it through the side windows and in the rear-view mirror.

Being an individual who didn't panic easily, the secretary continued to drive but she noticed that her car would not accelerate. Moreover, she felt as if the mysterious object was actually doing the steering. After hovering over the car for several miles the UFO moved away, becoming redder as it did so. From a distance it resembled a glowing, inverted mushroom with a short stem on top and two bright white lights and several smaller ones on the bottom. During the sighting the UFO made no sound.

After her encounter with the UFO, the secretary found several things wrong with her car: The radio was weak, the oil gauge was stuck, the battery would not charge properly and the speedometer readings were too low. She had noticed none of these malfunctions previously.

When the Colorado Project received a report on the case, its investigators decided to concentrate on the possibility that the UFO had caused the car to malfunction. After the witness was interviewed the Comet was taken to Dearborn, Michigan, where Ford engineers examined it thoroughly. They found that the radio malfunction was due to a broken antenna. An electrical leakage was responsible for the stuck oil gauge. The trouble with the battery began with a loose fan belt that was slowing the operation of the car's generator. And the speedometer had a broken part. All these defects, said the Ford engineers, could be expected in a car of the Comet's age and mileage. They found no evidence that the UFO was responsible in any way.

This case went into the Colorado Project's files as "unexplained." Although her car provided no evidence of the presence of a UFO, the report from the observer was complete and, in most respects, reliable. It was one of the few sightings for which no plausible explanation could be found when detailed information was available.

In January 1969, the Colorado Project issued a 1,465-page report entitled *Scientific Study of Unidentified Flying Objects.*

127

In addition to case studies, the report contains much of the technical and scientific material relating to UFOs that the Project studied in the course of its investigation.

In Section 1 of the *Scientific Study of Unidentified Flying Objects,* Dr. Condon sums up the Project's conclusion about UFOs: "Our general conclusion is that nothing has come from the study of UFOs in the past 21 years that has added to scientific knowledge." And he adds: "Further extensive study of UFOs probably cannot be justified in the expectation that science will be advanced thereby."

Dr. Condon does not recommend that all study of UFOs cease, however. Clearly defined, specific proposals by trained scientists for research, especially in possible UFO-related subjects such as atmospheric electricity, should receive consideration, he says. But he feels that the chances of worthwhile results are small at the present time.

Nowhere in its many pages does the *Scientific Study of Unidentified Flying Objects* deny that UFOs exist. But it does state emphatically that there is no evidence that they could be of interstellar or interplanetary origin. Instead, the report suggests that an explanation will eventually be found through increased knowledge of little-understood phenomena.

Like everything else connected with UFOs, the *Scientific Study of Unidentified Flying Objects* aroused heated controversy. The review panel chosen by the National Academy of Sciences announced that the study was a "very creditable effort to apply objectively the relevant techniques of science to the solution of the UFO problem."

On the other hand, NICAP was highly critical of the report's conclusions as well as the Colorado Project's selection and investigation of UFO cases. The atmospheric physicist, Dr. James E. McDonald, claimed that the contents of the report failed to support Dr. Condon's conclusions. To Dr. J. Allen Hynek, the Air Force UFO consultant, the percentage of unexplained UFOs in the Colorado report seemed to be higher than in the Project Blue Book investigation. Dr. Hynek recommended that the report not be the last word on UFOs.

Unless human nature changes drastically or all unexplained UFO sightings can somehow be explained, the chances are that the *Scientific Study of Unidentified Flying Objects* will *not* be the last word on the subject.

10

If You See
a UFO

According to opinion surveys, several million Americans believe that they have seen UFOs, and this number will increase. Every year there are more man-made objects such as airplanes and balloons in the skies above this and other countries and not all of them are recognized as airplanes or balloons. Planets, meteors and various natural phenomena present identification problems, too.

The chances are that sooner or later you will see something in the sky that you cannot immediately identify. When that happens, it is well to remember that all but a small percentage of UFOs turn out to be common objects or natural phenomena of one kind or another. When you see a flying object that puzzles you, you should ask yourself: "Could it be an airplane or a balloon?" Many new types of aircraft are in operation and some of them display unusual lights when flying at night. Also, certain weather conditions can

What appears to be a mysterious, wingless, cigar-shaped flying object is actually a B-36 bomber. U.S. Air Force

cause aircraft to look like flying discs or wingless cigar-shaped objects.

A silvery, transparent, flying disc may be a balloon, especially if there is no exhaust or engine noise and no visible means of propulsion. Balloons can travel to great heights where they reflect sunlight when the sun is below the horizon. Experimental balloons are sometimes released in clusters and they can be mistaken for UFOs flying in formation or hovering in a group. However, if the objects that you see are

131

traveling very fast or moving against the wind, they are probably not balloons.

If you should observe a bright, saucer-shaped object near the horizon that seems to change color and move, remember that Venus, Jupiter and Mars are bright planets that appear to do just that when they are observed through haze or mist. If you look at one of these planets long enough without a good point of reference, you might think that it is an erratically maneuvering UFO. An almanac will tell you when the

Contrails left by high-flying aircraft (white streak in photo) have been the cause of many UFO reports.   U.S. Air Force

This photo of the 1957 comet, Mrkos, illustrates how comets can easily be mistaken for unidentified flying objects. U.S. Air Force

planets appear low on the horizon as morning and evening stars.

Each year the earth passes through several meteor showers and during those periods the number of UFO reports always increases. Meteors are bits of material from space that enter the earth's atmosphere where they become so intensely heated that they turn into incandescent gas. Meteors appear in a variety of colors, shapes and sizes. They usually remain

133

in sight less than ten seconds. Meteors can travel in clusters, giving the appearance of UFOs in formation, or they can appear to follow a path parallel to the horizon which makes them look like a slow-moving UFO. Meteor showers occur at regular intervals. The Lyrids, for example, can be observed on or about April 20 each year and the Perseids around August 10. An astronomy text will have the dates of other meteor showers. Isolated meteors can be seen throughout the year and they are often reported as UFOs.

If you see a bright object near the sun, it may be a sundog, caused by sunlight reflecting from a layer of flat ice crystals. If the phenomenon occurs near the moon, it is called a moondog. Both sundogs and moondogs have been reported as UFOs.

When you see something that might be a UFO, remember that unusual atmospheric conditions can transform a common, everyday object into something that looks quite different. Car lights reflecting on clouds can create darting, luminous discs. Stars and planets may appear to change color when seen through water droplets and ice particles in the atmosphere. During temperature inversions, objects on the ground may seem to be floating in the sky.

Finally, your own physiological and psychological state may affect your interpretation of what you see. People who are very tired or under a strain are apt to make mistakes in identification. If they have been reading about UFOs or hearing stories about them, and they are susceptible to suggestion, they can transform almost any unfamiliar airborne object into a UFO. To guard against this tendency, try to evaluate your sighting objectively. Your own state of mind

Sundogs caused by the reflection of the sun's rays on a flat layer of ice crystals have been mistaken for unidentified flying objects. This photograph of a sundog (bright object, lower left) was taken over Indiana in 1954. U.S. Air Force

can be as important to the accuracy of your observation as your knowledge of any unusual atmospheric conditions that might be present.

When you do see something in the sky that you cannot immediately identify, you will want to know what to observe. If you report your sighting and your observations are accurate, it will be easier for investigators to identify your UFO. It may turn out to be a familiar object that you didn't recognize. Or you may see a true UFO, one of those rare sightings that cannot be identified as any known object or phenomenon.

Here are some things to note if you see an object that you think might be a UFO. The items listed below were included in the list the Air Force used when it was investigating and analyzing UFO reports:

   a. Description of the Object or Objects:
- (1) Shape.
- (2) Size compared to a known object.
- (3) Color.
- (4) Number.
- (5) Formation, if more than one.
- (6) Any discernible features or details.
- (7) Tail, trail, exhaust, including size of same compared to size of object.
- (8) Sound.
- (9) Other pertinent or unusual features.

   b. Description of Course of Object or Objects:
- (1) What first called the attention of observer to the object?
- (2) Angle of elevation and azimuth of object when

first observed. (Use theodolite or compass measurement if possible.)

(3) Angle of elevation and azimuth of object upon disappearance. (Use theodolite or compass measurement if possible.)

(4) Description of flight path and maneuvers of object. (Use elevations and azimuth, not altitude.)

(5) How did the object disappear? (Instantaneously to the north, etc.)

(6) How long was the object visible? (Be specific, 5 minutes, 1 hour, etc.)

If you should be lucky enough to photograph a UFO and you wish to use your photographs as evidence of your sighting, you should be prepared to supply some information along with the prints and negatives. In addition to basic data on place, time and date, the following information will be useful:

(1) Type and make of camera.

(2) Type, focal length and make of lens.

(3) Brand and type of film.

(4) Shutter speed used.

(5) Lens opening used: that is, "f" stop.

(6) Filters used.

(7) Was tripod or solid stand used?

(8) Was panning used?

(9) Exact direction camera was pointing with relation to true north, and its angle with respect to the ground.

Since December 1969, when it terminated Project Blue Book, the Air Force has not investigated UFO reports. The ending of the investigations had been recommended by the Colorado Project and the Air Force agreed that Project Blue Book could no longer be justified for reasons of national security or in the interest of science. None of its investigations had uncovered any threat to the United States, the Air Force said. Its investigators had found no technical developments unknown to scientists and no evidence that any of the sightings were extraterrestrial vehicles.

Although the Air Force no longer investigates UFO reports, a citizen who sees an object in the sky that he cannot identify can call the nearest air base to determine if the object has been seen, and identified, there. Civilian UFO groups continue to conduct investigations and many reports are made to them. UFOs are also reported to police, town or city officials, newspapers, radio and TV stations and, sometimes, to no one other than family and friends. Most of these sightings can be explained, of course. The few that cannot be explained are true UFOs and they are strange and mysterious things, indeed. Someday, perhaps, scientists will be able to tell us more about them.

Bibliography

CHAMBERS, HOWARD V. *UFOs for the Millions.* New York: Bell, 1967.
DAVID, JAY, ed. *The Flying Saucer Reader.* New York: New
American Library, Signet Books, 1967.
FULLER, JOHN G. *Aliens in the Skies: the New UFO Battle of the
Scientists.* New York: G. P. Putnam's Sons, Berkley Medallion
Books, 1969.
FULLER, JOHN G. *Incident at Exeter.* New York: G. P. Putnam's Sons,
Berkley Medallion Books, 1966.
KEYHOE, DONALD E. *Flying Saucers from Outer Space.* New York:
Henry Holt & Co., 1953.
KLASS, PHILIP J. *UFOs—Identified.* New York: Random House, 1968.
LORENZEN, JIM and CORAL LORENZEN. *UFOs Over the Americas.*
New York: New American Library, Signet Books, 1968.
MALLAN, LLOYD. *The Official Guide to UFOs.* New York:
Science & Mechanics Publishing Co., 1967.
MENZEL, DONALD H. and LYLE G. BOYD. *The World of Flying
Saucers.* Garden City, N. Y.: Doubleday, 1963.
MICHEL, AIMÉ. *The Truth About Flying Saucers.* New York:
Pyramid Publications, Pyramid Books, 1956.
NATIONAL INVESTIGATIONS COMMITTEE ON AERIAL PHENOMENA.
The UFO Evidence. Washington: NICAP, 1964.
OGLES, GEORGE W. "What Does the Air Force Really Know About
Flying Saucers?" *Airman* magazine, July, August, 1967.
RUBLOWSKY, JOHN. *Is Anybody Out There?* New York: Walker, 1962.
RUPPELT, EDWARD J. *The Report on Unidentified Flying Objects.*
Garden City, N. Y.: Doubleday, 1956.
SAUNDERS, DAVID R. and R. ROGER HARKINS. *UFOs? Yes!* New York:
New American Library, Signet Books, 1969.
SULLIVAN, WALTER. *We Are Not Alone.* New York: McGraw-Hill,
1966.
U. S. LIBRARY OF CONGRESS LEGISLATIVE REFERENCE SERVICE.
Facts About Unidentified Flying Objects. Washington: Library of
Congress, 1966.
U. S. SUPT. OF DOCUMENTS. *Aids to Identification of Flying Objects.*
Washington: U. S. Government Printing Office, 1968.
UNIVERSITY OF COLORADO. *Scientific Study of Unidentified Flying
Objects.* New York: Bantam Books, 1969.
WHITE, DALE. *Is Something Up There?* Garden City, N. Y.:
Doubleday, 1968.
YOUNG, MORT. *UFO: Top Secret.* New York: Simon & Schuster,
Essandess Special Editions, 1967.

Index